PADMASAMBHAVA COMES TO TIBET

Padmasambhava Comes to Tibet

25 DISCIPLES – VAJRA GURU MANTRA – PRAYERS

Yeshe Tsogyal

WITH INTRODUCTIONS AND CONTRIBUTIONS BY

Tarthang Tulku

DHARMA PUBLISHING

TIBETAN TRANSLATION SERIES

For information, contact
2425 Hillside Ave., Berkeley, California, 94704 USA

Edited by the staff of Dharma Publishing
Typeset in Jenson with Voluta Script headings
Printed and bound in the United States of America
by Dharma Press, Ratna Ling, California
Design and layout by Kando Dorsey

Library of Congress Control Number: 2008943677

ISBN 13: 978-0-89800-437-3

Frontispiece: 'Nga Dra Ma', the statue
Padmasambhava named 'Same as Me'

Dharma Publishing is also the publisher of
Life and Liberation of Padmasambhava, vols 1–2

9 8 7 6 5 4 3 2 1

Dedication

From the vast ocean of enlightened qualities of the Trikāya—Dharmakāya Amitābha, Sambhogakāya Avalokiteshvara, and Nirmāṇakāya Padmasambhava—a few small droplets have been collected together to create this volume. May this publication offer a glimpse of the light of liberation, which has now, according to predictions, just begun to shine in the West, the Land of the Red-faced Ones, some 2500 years after the era of Shākyamuni Buddha.

We enter the Dharma by making the acquaintance of the Enlightened Ones, the finest examples and guides to the complete teachings of the Buddhas of the past, present, and future. This book is dedicated to all who read about the life and liberation of the Great Guru Padmasambhava. May his blessing fill their hearts with faith, love, and joy. And may the ancient lineages of light shine upon the West and all the world for countless generations to come.

Tarthang Tulku

After I have passed into Parinirvāṇa,
when two years short of a decade come to pass,
the most supreme Victor Over All the World,
known as the Lotus-born One of Oḍḍiyāna,
will be born from a lotus to teach
the Secret Mantrayāna.
Thus I prophesy.

Prophecy by Śākyamuni Buddha

GURU RINPOCHE

Table of Contents

Trikāya White Lotus Blossom, King of Wish-fulfilling Gems
by Tarthang Tulku
13

Padmasambhava Comes to Tibet
by Yeshe Tsogyal
69

Twenty-five Disciples of Padmasambhava
135

Vajra Guru Mantra
199

Prayers
227

Index
278

Trikāya White Lotus Blossom, King of Wish-fulfilling Gems

HOMAGE TO THE LOTUS-BORN GURU OF OḌḌIYĀNA

༄༅།། སྐུ་གསུམ་པད་དཀར་བཞད་པ་ཡིད་བཞིན་དབང་གི་རྒྱལ་པོ།།

ན་མོ་གུ་རུ་བྷྱེ༔

བདེ་ཆེན་ཞིང་དུ་མགོན་པོ་སྣང་མཐའ་ཡས།།

རི་བོ་ཏ་ལར་འཕགས་མཆོག་སྤྱན་རས་གཟིགས།།

ཨོ་རྒྱན་མཚོ་གླིང་པདྨ་འབྱུང་གནས་ཞེས།།

སྐུ་གསུམ་དབྱེར་མེད་བླ་མར་གུས་ཕྱག་འཚལ།།

དེ་ལ་ཨོ་རྒྱན་གྱི་སློབ་དཔོན་ཆེན་པོ་པདྨ་འབྱུང་གནས་ཀྱི་སྐུ་ཆེ་བའི་
ཡོན་ཏན་ཚུ་ཐིགས་ཙམ་ཞིག་བརྗོད་ན།

འཇམ་དཔལ་སྒྱུ་འཕྲུལ་དྲྭ་བ་ལས།
དཔལ་ལྡན་སངས་རྒྱས་པདྨ་སྐྱེས།།
ཀུན་མཁྱེན་ཡེ་ཤེས་མཛོད་འཛིན་པ།།
རྒྱལ་པོ་སྒྱུ་འཕྲུལ་སྣ་ཚོགས་འཆང་།།
ཆེ་བ་སངས་རྒྱས་རིག་སྔགས་འཆང་།།
ཞེས་དང་།

དུས་གསུམ་སངས་རྒྱས་ཀུན་གྱི་ཕྲིན་ལས་བདག།
མཉམ་མེད་ཀུན་བཟང་རྡོ་རྗེ་འཆང་ཆེན་པོ།།
སྤྲུལ་པའི་སྐུར་སྣང་ཐུགས་རྗེ་ཆེན་པོར་ལྡན།།
གང་ལ་གང་འདུལ་ཕྲིན་ལས་རླབས་པོ་ཆེ།།

སེམས་ཅན་ཀུན་གྱི་རེ་འདོད་ཡིད་བཞིན་སྐོང་།།
ཞེས་གསུངས་པ་ལྟར།

སངས་རྒྱས་མཆོག་གི་སྤྲུལ་སྐུ་གཅིག་གི་གདུལ་ཞིང་སྟོང་གསུམ་མི་མཇེད་ཀྱི་འཇིག་རྟེན་ན་འཛམ་གླིང་བྱེ་བ་ཕྲག་བརྒྱ་ཡོད་དོ།།

ཞིང་དེའི་སྟོན་པ་ཤཱཀྱ་ཐུབ་པ་བྱེ་བ་ཕྲག་བརྒྱས་རྒྱུ་མཚན་ཉིད་ཐེག་པའི་ཆོས་འཁོར་གཙོ་བོར་བསྐོར་ཞིང་། དེ་བཞིན་དུ་གུ་རུ་པདྨ་འབྱུང་གནས་བྱེ་བ་ཕྲག་བརྒྱས་འབྲས་བུ་གསང་སྔགས་རྡོ་རྗེ་ཐེག་པའི་ཆོས་ཀྱི་འཁོར་ལོ་བསྐོར་ཏོ།།

དེ་གཉིས་ཀ་རྣམ་འགྱུར་ཐ་དད་ཀྱང་ངོ་བོ་ཐ་མི་དད་ཅིང་ཡེ་ཤེས་གཅིག་གི་རྣམ་རོལ་ཏུ་སྒྱུར་པ་ཁོ་ན་ཡིན་ནོ།།

ཇི་སྐད་དུ།

ཆོས་དབྱིངས་གནས་སུ་ཀུན་ཏུ་བཟང་པོ་དང༔

སྟུག་པོ་བཀོད་དུ་རྡོ་རྗེ་འཆང་ཆེན་པོ༔

རྡོ་རྗེ་གདན་དུ་ཐུབ་པ་ཆེན་པོ་ཉིད༔

གཉིས་མེད་པདྨ་ར་ལྷུན་ཀྱིས་གྲུབ༔

ཅེས་དང་།

རང་བྱུང་པདྨ་ཞེས་བྱར་གྲགས་པ་ད༔

སངས་རྒྱས་སྣང་བ་མཐའ་ཡས་ཐུགས་ལས་རྡོལ༔

ཐུགས་རྗེ་སྤྱན་རས་གཟིགས་དབང་གསུང་ལས་སྤྲུལ༔

མཁའ་འགྲོ་ཡོངས་ཀྱི་མིང་པོ་དཔའ་བོ་རྒྱལ༔

མཉམ་མེད་ཀུན་བཟང་རྡོ་རྗེ་འཆང་ཆེན་པོ༔

སྤྲུལ་པའི་སྐུར་སྣང་ཐུགས་རྗེ་ཆེན་པོར་ལྡན༔

ཞེས་དང་།

མདོ་སྡེ་མྱང་འདས་ལས།

ང་ནི་ཡོངས་སུ་མྱ་ངན་འདའོ།།

ཁྱེད་རྣམས་མྱ་ངན་མ་བྱེད་ཅིག།

མདངས་ལྡན་དྲི་མེད་མཚོ་དཀྱིལ་ནས།།

ང་ལས་ལྷག་པའི་སྐྱེས་བུ་འབྱུང་།།

ཞེས་དང་།

དབུས་འགྱུར་འཆང་ལུང་བསྟན་པའི་མདོ་སྡེ་ལས།

ང་ནི་འདི་ནས་མི་སྣང་ནས།།

ལོ་ནི་བཞི་གཉིས་ལོན་པ་ན།།

ཨོ་རྒྱན་ཡུལ་གྱི་ནུབ་བྱང་མཚམས།།

དྷ་ན་ཀོ་ཤའི་མཚོ་གླིང་དུ།།

ཀུན་ལས་ལྷག་པའི་སྐྱེས་བུ་འབྱུང་།།

ཞེས་དང་།

ཨོཾ་ཨཱཿཧཱུྃ་བཛྲ་གུ་རུ་པདྨ་སིདྡྷི་ཧཱུྃ

བླ་མེད་དོན་རྫོགས་འདུས་པའི་རྒྱུད་ལས།

ང་ནི་མྱ་ངན་འདས་འོག་ཏུ།།

ལོ་ནི་བཅུ་རུ་གཉིས་ཚད་ན།།

འཇིག་རྟེན་ཀུན་ལས་རྒྱལ་བ་མཆོག།

ཨོ་རྒྱན་ཡུལ་དུ་པད་འབྱུང་ཞེས།།

པདྨ་ལས་ནི་འབྱུང་བར་འགྱུར།།

གསང་སྔགས་སྟོན་པར་ངེས་ལུང་བསྟན།།

ཞེས་སོགས་གསུངས་ཤིང་།

དེ་ཡང་ཕྱོགས་བཅུའི་རྒྱལ་བ་ཐམས་ཅད་འགྲོ་དོན་ལ་བཞེངས་པའི་དགོངས་དབྱངས་ནི་གཅིག་ཏུ་མཐུན།   སྐུ་གསུང་ཐུགས་ཡོན་འཕྲིན་ལས་མི་ཟད་པ་རྒྱན་གྱི་འཁོར་ལོའི་ངོ་བོ་ཡོད་དོ་ཅོག་ནི་གཅིག་ཏུ་འདུས་པ།   སངས་རྒྱས་སྣང་བ་མཐའ་ཡས་ཀྱི་ཐུགས་ཀར་ཐིམ་པ་ལས།   ཐུགས་འཇའ་འོད་ཚོན་རིན་ཆེན་ཟ་མ་ཏོག་ཁ་ཕྱེ་བའི་ནང་

ནས། གསེར་གྱི་རྡོ་རྗེ་ཧྲཱིཿས་མཚན་པ་འོད་ཟེར་ལྔ་ལྡན་རང་འབར་བ་ཞིག་བྱོན་ཏེ།

སིནྡྷུ་འོ་མ་ཅན་གྱི་རྒྱ་མཚོ་དྷ་ན་ཀོ་ཤའི་དབུས་སུ་པདྨའི་སྡོང་པོ་མཆོག་ཏུ་རྒྱས་པའི་གེ་སར་གྱི་རྩེར་བབས་པ་འོད་དུ་ཞུ་ནས།

མཚན་དཔེ་གསལ་རྫོགས་ཡེ་ཤེས་ཀྱི་སྐུ་ཅན་རིག་པ་ཐོལ་སྐྱེས་ཀྱི་ཚུལ་དུ་ཤིན་ཏུ་མཛེས་པ་གསལ་འཚེར་ལྷུན་སྡུག་གི་སྐུ་མཆོག མངལ་གྱིས་མ་གོས་པར་མཚོ་སྐྱེས་རྡོ་རྗེའི་སྐུ་མཚན་དཔེའི་པད་མོ་རྣམ་པར་བཞད་དོ།།

དེའི་ཚེ་ཕྱོགས་བཅུའི་སངས་རྒྱས་ཐམས་ཅད་ཀྱིས་དགོངས་པས་ནི་མངའ་གསོལ་ཞིང་དབང་བསྐུར།

བྱང་ཆུབ་སེམས་དཔའ་དང་སེམས་མའི་ཚོགས་མ་ལུས་པས་འགྲོ་

ཨོཾ་ཨཱཿཧཱུྃ་བཛྲ་གུ་རུ་པདྨ་སིདྡྷི་ཧཱུྃ།

དོན་མཛད་པའི་གྲོགས་དང་མཐུན་འགྱུར་ལ་ནི་གཅིག་ཏུ་གསོལ། གནས་གསུམ་གྱི་དཔའ་བོ་དང་མཁའ་འགྲོ་མ་རྣམས་ཀྱིས་གཟིངས་བསྐྱོད་ཀྱི་ལས་ལ་ནི་གཅིག་ཏུ་བྲེལ་ཏེ་བཞུགས་པ་ལ། ཨོ་རྒྱན་གྱི་རྒྱལ་པོ་ཨིནྡྲ་བོ་དྷིའི་སྲས་ཀྱི་སྐལ་བར་སྨིན་དྲངས་ནས།

རྒྱལ་སྲིད་ཕུལ་བ་རེ་ཞིག་བཞེས་ཚུལ་བསྟན་ནས་རྒྱལ་སྲིད་ཆོས་བཞིན་བསྐྱངས་སོ།།

ཐབས་མཁས་ཀྱི་མཛད་པ་རྣམ་པ་དུ་མས་སླར་ཡང་རྒྱལ་སྲིད་མཆིལ་མའི་ཐལ་བ་བཞིན་སྤངས་ཏེ།

སློབ་དཔོན་ཆེན་པོ་པྲ་བྷ་ཧསྟིའི་སྤྱན་སྔར་རབ་ཏུ་བྱུང་། ས་ཡི་ལྷ་མོས་ཕུལ་བའི་ངུར་སྨྲིག་གི་ཆོས་གོས་བཞེས། ཕྱོགས་བཅུའི་སངས་རྒྱས་རྣམས་མངོན་སུམ་དུ་ནམ་མཁའ་ནས་བྱོན་ཏེ་ལེགས་སོ་

ཞེས་མངའ་གསོལ་མཛད་དེ་ཤཱཀྱའི་དགེ་སློང་སུ་མི་ཏྲ་ཞེས་བྱ་བའི་མཚན་གྱིས་སྒྲ་བར་གྱུར་ཏོ།།

དེ་ནས་བཅོམ་ལྡན་འདས་ཤཱཀྱ་ཐུབ་པའི་ཉེ་གནས་གནས་བརྟན་ཀུན་དགའ་བོའི་སྤྱན་སྔར་ཕེབས་ཏེ།

ལོ་ལྔའི་བར་དུ་ཉིན་མཚན་ཁོར་ཡུག་ཏུ་རྒྱུ་མཚན་ཉིད་ཐེག་པའི་ཆོས་དོན་མ་ལུས་པ་སྦྱངས་པའི་ཚུལ་མཛད་དོ།།

དེ་ནས་མཁའ་འགྲོ་མ་ལས་ཀྱི་དབང་མོ་ཆེ་ལས་ཕྱི་ནང་གསང་བའི་དབང་བསྐུར་རྫོགས་པར་ཞུས་ཏེ།

གསང་སྔགས་ཕྱི་ནང་གི་རྒྱུད་སྡེ་ཐམས་ཅད་ཐུགས་སུ་ཆུད།
སློབ་དཔོན་འཇམ་དཔལ་བཤེས་གཉེན་སོགས་གྲུབ་པའི་རིག་འཛིན་ཆེན་པོ་བརྒྱད་ལས།

སྒྲུབ་སྡེ་བཀའ་བརྒྱད་ཀྱི་རྒྱུད་སྡེ་དང་སྒྲུབ་སྡེ་ཐམས་ཅད་ཀྱི་སྨིན་ཅིང་
གྲོལ་བའི་བསྒྲུབ་པས་གྲུབ་པ་ཆེན་པོའི་རྟགས་ཐོན།

དུར་ཁྲོད་ཆེན་པོ་བརྒྱད་སོགས་སུ་མ་དང་མཁའ་འགྲོའི་ཚོགས་དང་
ཐབས་ཅིག་ཏུ་རིག་པ་བརྟུལ་ཞུགས་ཀྱི་སྤྱོད་པ་བསྐྱངས།

ཐོད་འཕྲེང་སྡེ་ལྔ་གུ་རུ་མཚན་བརྒྱད་ཐུབ་པ་དྲུག་འཕྲུལ་མཚན་
བཞི་བཅུ།

རྒྱན་དྲུག་མཆོག་གཉིས་གྲུབ་ཆེན་བརྒྱད་ཅུ་རྩ་བཞི་སོགས་སྒྲུབ་
པའི་རྣམ་རོལ་བསམ་གྱིས་མི་ཁྱབ་པས།

རྒྱ་གར་འཕགས་ཡུལ་སོགས་སུ་མདོ་སྔགས་ཀྱི་བསྟན་པ་ཡོངས་
རྫོགས་འཛིན་སྐྱོང་སྤེལ་བའི་འཕྲིན་ལས་ཆེན་པོས་ཕན་བདེའི་ཉི་མ་
ཤར་བར་མཛད།

སྤྲུལ་སྐུ་དགའ་རབ་རྡོ་རྗེ་དང་རིག་འཛིན་ཤྲཱི་སིངྷ་སོགས་ལས་ཐེག་དགུའི་རྩེ་རྒྱལ་མན་ངག་རྫོགས་པ་ཆེན་པོའི་ཆོས་བཀའ་རྒྱ་མཚོ་ལྟ་བུ་ཟབ་ཅིང་ཡངས་པ་ཐུགས་སུ་ཆུབ་པར་གྱུར་ཏེ།

སླར་ཡང་ནུབ་ཕྱོགས་ས་ཧོར་ཡུལ་དུ་མེ་དཔུང་མཚོ་རུ་འཁྱིལ་བའི་དབུས་སུ་པདྨའི་སྡོང་པོའི་རྩེར་བཞུགས་པ་སོགས་རྫུ་འཕྲུལ་ཡ་མ་ཟླང་གི་བཀོད་པ་སྣ་ཚོགས་བསམ་གྱིས་མི་ཁྱབ་པས་གདུལ་བྱ་རྣམས་རང་དབང་མེད་པར་དད་པའི་གནས་ལ་བཀོད་དེ།

སྐྱེ་འགྲོ་ཐམས་ཅད་ཆོས་ལ་བཙུད་ནས་ཕྱིར་མི་ལྡོག་པའི་ས་ལ་བཞག་སྟེ། པདྨ་ཐོད་ཕྲེང་རྩལ་དུ་གྲགས།

དེ་ནས་རྒྱབ་འགྱུར་ཚལ་དུ་རྡོ་རྗེ་ཕག་མོའི་བྱིན་གྱིས་བརླབས་ཏེ་ཀླུ་དང་གཟའ་སྐར་ཐམས་ཅད་དམ་ལ་བཏགས།

གནས་གསུམ་གྱི་དཔའ་བོ་མཁའ་འགྲོ་མ་རྣམས་ཀྱིས་དངོས་གྲུབ་སྩོལ་ཏེ་རྡོ་རྗེ་དྲག་པོ་རྩལ་དུ་གྲགས།

དེ་ནས་རྡོ་རྗེ་གདན་དུ་མུ་སྟེགས་སྟོན་པ་ལྔ་བརྒྱས་རྩོད་པ་རྩོམ་པའི་ཚེ་ཐོག་ཆེན་ཕབ་ནས་བསྒྲལ། ལྷག་མ་སངས་རྒྱས་ཀྱི་བསྟན་པ་བཙུད་པས་སེངྒེ་སྒྲ་སྒྲོག་ཏུ་གསོལ།

དེ་ནས་བོད་ཁམས་འདུལ་བ་དང་མཁན་སློབ་ཆོས་རྒྱལ་ཞལ་འཛོམས་པའི་རྟེན་འབྲེལ་དུས་བབས་སུ་གཟིགས་ནས།
ཛམ་གླིང་ཆོས་ཀྱི་རྒྱལ་པོ་ཁྲི་སྲོང་ལྡེའུ་བཙན་གྱི་སྤྱན་འདྲེན་པོ་ཉའི་ཕེབས་བསུ་དང་བསྟུན།

བོད་ཡུལ་གངས་ཅན་ལྗོངས་སུ་རིམ་གྱིས་ཕེབས་ཤིང་ཕེབས་ལམ་དུ་བརྟན་མ་བཅུ་གཉིས། སྐྱོང་མ་བཅུ་གཉིས། མགར་ལྷ་བཅུ་གསུམ། དགེ་བསྙེན་ཉེར་གཅིག་སོགས་མི་མ་ཡིན་ཐུ་བོ་ཆེ་རྣམས་

དམ་ལ་བཏགས་ཤིང་བསྟན་པ་སྲུང་བའི་བཀའ་སྡོད་དུ་བསྐོས།

སྡོད་ལུང་གཞོང་པ་ལྷ་ཚུ་བརྟེན་པ་དང་རྫུ་འཕྲུལ་གྱི་མེས་ང་ཚེ་རྒྱལ་པོའི་ཐུགས་རྒྱལ་བཅོམ་པས་མཚོན་ཏེ་གྲུབ་པའི་སྤྱོད་པ་མཐའ་ཡས་པས་བོད་ཀྱི་གདུལ་བྱ་རྣམས་བཏུལ།

སྣང་སྲིད་ཀྱི་ལྷ་མ་སྲིན་སྡེ་བརྒྱད་ལ་བཀའ་བསྒྲོས་ཤིང་དམ་ལ་བཏགས་ཏེ། བསམ་ཡས་མི་འགྱུར་ལྷུན་གྱིས་གྲུབ་པའི་གཙུག་ལག་ཁང་ཆེན་པོ་རྟེན་དང་བརྟེན་པར་བཅས་པ།

རྫུ་འཕྲུལ་གྱིས་ལོ་ལྔའི་ཁོངས་སུ་ལེགས་པར་བཞེངས།

རབ་གནས་མཛད་པའི་ཚེ་སྐྱེ་རྒུ་རྣམས་ཀྱི་དད་པའི་སྣང་བ་ཚོས་ལ་སྐད་ཅིག་གིས་འགྱུར་ཏེ།

དག་སྣང་འབྱུང་བ་མེད་པའི་དཔལ་ཤིན་ཏུ་རྒྱས་ཤིང་ཆོས་ཀྱི་སྒྲོན་མེ་སྦར་བའི་སྒོ་ཆེན་ཕྱེ་བར་མཛད་དེ།

བཀའ་བབས་ཐུགས་ཀྱི་བུ་དགུ་སོགས་སློབ་ཅིང་གྲོལ་བར་མཛད་ནས་སྟན་ཐོག་གཅིག་ཏུ་རིག་འཛིན་གྲུབ་པའི་གོ་འཕང་མཐོན་པོ་ལ་བཀོད་པ་སོགས།

བོད་ཀྱི་མི་དང་མི་མ་ཡིན་གྱི་སློབ་ཚོགས་ནམ་མཁའི་སྐར་ཕྲེང་ལྟར་བྱུང་ཞིང་། སྒྲུབ་གྲྭ་དང་སྒོམ་གྲྭས་བོད་ཀྱི་རི་སུལ་ཀུན་ཁྱབ་པར་མཛད་ཅིང་།

གྲགས་པའི་མཚོ་ཆེན་བཞི། ཕུག་ཆེན་བཞི། སྦས་གནས་རྒྱལ་པོ་བཞི་སོགས་རི་བྲག་ཐམས་ཅད་རིག་འཛིན་གྲུབ་པའི་གནས་སུ་བྱིན་གྱིས་བརླབས་པ་སོགས།

གང་ལ་གང་འདུལ་སྤྲུལ་པའི་རོལ་གར་གྱིས་མཛད་པ་

འདི་ལྟར་སྟོན་ཏེ།

འགྲོ་འདུལ་དགོངས་མཛད་པདྨའི་ལྷུམས་ཞུགས་མཛད།།

རང་བྱུང་བལྟམས་མཛད་རྒྱལ་སྲས་རོལ་རྩེད་མཛད།།

རབ་ཏུ་བྱུང་མཛད་དཀའ་ཐུབ་སྣ་ཚོགས་མཛད།།

བདུད་དཔུང་འཛོམས་མཛད་སངས་རྒྱས་བྱང་ཆུབ་མཛད།།

ཆོས་འཁོར་བསྐོར་མཛད་བརྟུལ་ཞུགས་སྤྱོད་པ་མཛད།།

བསྟན་པ་མཐར་རྒྱས་མི་ནུབ་གཏེར་སྦས་མཛད།།

ཅེས་དང་།

གུ་རུའི་རྣམ་ཐར་རྒྱས་བསྡུས་གང་འཐད་པ།།

མཐོང་ཐོས་མོས་གུས་ཚད་མེད་བྱ་བ་གཅེས།།

འདི་ལ་དད་པས་ཐར་པའི་རྒྱལ་ས་ཟིན།།
བླ་མེད་བྱང་ཆུབ་འཚང་རྒྱ་ཐེ་ཚོམ་མེད།།
ཅེས་དང་།

ཨུ་རྒྱན་རྣམ་ཐར་མདོར་བསྡུས་མཛད་པ་ནི།།
སུ་ཡིས་བྲིས་སམ་མཐོང་ཐོས་གཞན་ལ་སྟོན།།
དེ་དག་བདེ་བ་ཅན་གྱི་ཞིང་དུ་སྐྱེ།།
འདི་ལ་དད་ཅིང་མོས་པས་སྤྱོད་ཚད་རྣམས།།
བླ་མེད་སངས་རྒྱས་ཐོབ་པར་ཐེ་ཚོམ་མེད།།
ཅེས་གསུངས་སོ།།

ཆེད་དུ་བརྗོད་པའི་ཚིགས་སུ་བཅད་པ་ནི།

ཕྱོགས་བཅུའི་རྒྱལ་བ་རབ་འབྱམས་མ་ལུས་པའི།།
སྐུ་གསུང་ཐུགས་ཡོན་ཕྲིན་ལས་གཅིག་བསྡུས་ནས།།
འོད་དཔག་མེད་པའི་ཐུགས་ཀར་ཐིམ་པ་ན།།
དེ་ཐུགས་རིན་ཆེན་འོད་ལྡའི་ཟ་མ་ཏོག།

ཁ་ཕྱེ་ནང་ནས་ཧྲཱིཿཡིག་འོད་ལྡ་ཡི།།
མདངས་འབར་ཨོ་རྒྱན་ཡུལ་གྱི་ནུབ་བྱང་མཚམས།།
རྒྱ་མཚོ་དྲི་མེད་མདངས་ལྡན་འཁྱིངས་པའི་དབུས།།
རང་བྱུང་པདྨ་གེ་སར་སྡོང་པོའི་རྩེར།།

མ་དང་ཕ་ཡི་རྐྱེན་ལ་མ་ལྟོས་པས།།
མཚན་དང་དཔེ་བྱད་གསལ་རྫོགས་ལྷུན་གྱིས་གྲུབ།།
ངོ་མཚར་རང་བྱུང་འཇའ་ལུས་རྡོ་རྗེའི་སྐུ།།
རིག་པ་ཐོལ་སྐྱེས་ཚུལ་དུ་བལྟམས་པ་ན།།

ཕྱོགས་བཅུའི་སངས་རྒྱས་ཐམས་ཅད་དེར་བྱོན་ནས།།
ཟག་མེད་ཡེ་ཤེས་དགོངས་པས་དབང་ཡང་བསྐུར།།
བྱང་ཆུབ་སེམས་དཔའ་སེམས་མ་ཀུན་འདུས་ནས།།
འགྲོ་དོན་གྲོགས་དང་མཛད་པའི་དམ་བཅའ་ཕུར།།

གནས་གསུམ་དཔའ་བོ་ཌཱ་ཀི་སྲུང་མ་ཡིས།།
མངའ་གསོལ་གཟིངས་བསྟོད་ཤིས་པའི་རོལ་མོ་དཀྲོལ།།
དཀར་ཕྱོགས་སྐྱོང་བའི་ལྷ་ཀླུའི་ཚོགས་རྣམས་ཀྱི།།
ཕྱི་ནང་གསང་བའི་མཆོད་སྤྲིན་སྟོབས་པས་བྲེལ།།

དེ་ཚེ་ཨོ་རྒྱན་མཁའ་འགྲོའི་གླིང་ཆེན་མོའི༎
ཆོས་ཀྱི་རྒྱལ་པོ་འཁོར་ལོས་བསྒྱུར་བ་ནི༎
ཨིནྡྲ་བོ་དྷི་ཞེས་སུ་གྲགས་པའི་མཆོག༎
རྒྱ་མཚོར་ནོར་བུ་ལེན་དུ་བྱོན་པ་དང་༎

མཇལ་ཏེ་སྲས་ཀྱི་སྐལ་བར་གདན་དྲངས་ཤིང་༎
རྒྱལ་སྲིད་ཕུལ་བ་རེ་ཞིག་ཆོས་བཞིན་བསྐྱངས༎
སླར་ཡང་ཕྱོགས་བཅུའི་སངས་རྒྱས་བྱང་སེམས་དང་༎
གནས་གསུམ་དཔའ་བོ་མཁའ་འགྲོའི་ཚོགས་རྣམས་ཀྱིས༎

ཁབ་ནས་མངོན་པར་འབྱུང་བར་ལུང་གིས་བསྐུལ༎
ཐབས་མཁས་མཛད་སྤྱོད་དུ་མས་རྒྱལ་སྲིད་ནི༎
མཆིལ་མའི་ཐལ་བ་བཞིན་དུ་ཡོངས་སྤངས་ཏེ༎
པྲ་བྷ་ཧསྟིའི་སྤྱན་སྔར་རབ་བྱུང་སྟེ༎

ས་ཡི་ལྷ་མོས་དུར་ཁྲོད་ཞུལ་བ་བཞེས།།
དེ་ཚེ་མཁའ་ལས་རྒྱལ་རྣམས་ལེགས་སོ་གནང་།།
ཤཱཀྱའི་དགེ་སློང་སུ་མི་ཏྲ་རུ་གསོལ།།
མཚན་གཞན་གུ་རུ་ཤཱཀྱ་སེངྒེར་གྲགས།།

སངས་རྒྱས་ལུང་བསྟན་དབང་པོའི་སྡེ་ཡང་ཡིན།།
ཐུབ་པའི་ཉེ་གནས་དགྲ་བཅོམ་ཀུན་དགའ་བོའི།།
སྤྲིན་སྟར་ཞབས་ནས་མདོ་ཡི་དྲི་བ་མཛད།།
ལོ་ལྔའི་བར་དུ་ཉིན་མཚན་ཁོར་ཡུག་གིས།།

མཚན་ཉིད་རྒྱུ་ཡི་ཐེག་པ་ལ་སྦྱངས་ནས།།
ཚིག་དོན་མ་ལུས་ཁོངས་སུ་ཆུད་པར་མཛད།།
མཁའ་འགྲོའི་གཙོ་མོ་ལས་ཀྱི་དབང་མོ་ནས།།
གསང་སྔགས་ཕྱི་ནང་གསང་བའི་དབང་བསྐུར་གསན།།

དེ་ཚེ་ཕན་ཚུན་རྫུ་འཕྲུལ་ཅུང་འགྲན་ན།།
བླ་སློབ་མོས་གུས་རྟེན་འབྲེལ་འགྲིགས་པའི་མཐར།།
དེ་ཚེ་པད་འབྱུང་ཡི་གེ་ཧཱུྃ་དུ་བསྒྱུར།།
མཁའ་འགྲོས་མིད་ནས་ཁོང་པའི་ནང་རྒྱུད་དེ།།

གསང་བའི་པད་མོར་བཏོན་ཏེ་བྱིན་གྱིས་བརླབས།།
ཕྱི་ལྟར་སངས་རྒྱས་སྣང་བ་མཐའ་ཡས་སྐུ།།
ཚེ་ཡི་རིག་འཛིན་གྲུབ་པའི་དབང་རྣམས་ཐོབ།།
ནང་ལྟར་འཕགས་མཆོག་སྤྱན་རས་གཟིགས་ཀྱི་སྐུ།།

ཕྱག་རྒྱ་ཆེན་པོ་བསྒོམ་པའི་དབང་མཆོག་ཐོབ།།
གསང་བ་ལྟར་ན་རྟ་མགྲིན་དབང་གི་སྐུ།།
རྡིགས་པའི་ལྷ་འདྲེ་དམ་འདོགས་དབང་རྣམས་ཐོབ།།
གསང་ཆེན་རྒྱུད་སྡེའི་སྨིན་གྲོལ་རྒྱ་མཚོ་མནོས།།

འཇམ་དཔལ་བཤེས་གཉེན་ཀླུ་སྒྲུབ་སྙིང་པོ་སོགས།།
རིག་འཛིན་བརྒྱད་ལས་སྒྲུབ་སྡེའི་ཆོས་བཀའ་ཞུས།།
རིག་འཛིན་ཆེན་པོ་ཤྲཱི་སིངྷ་སོགས་ལས།།
རྫོགས་པ་ཆེན་པོའི་ཆོས་ལ་ཞུན་ཐར་བཅད།།

ཀུ་ཀུ་རཱ་ཛ་སོགས་ལས་བསམ་ཡས་སུ།།
གསང་སྔགས་རྒྱུད་སྡེ་རྒྱ་མཚོའི་སྨིན་གྲོལ་ཞུས།།
བསྒྲུབས་པས་གྲུབ་རྟགས་མ་ཐོན་འགའ་ཡང་མེད།།
ཚེ་དཔག་མེད་བསྒྲུབས་འཆི་མེད་རིག་འཛིན་ཐོབ།།

གང་གི་སྒྱུ་འཕྲུལ་རོལ་པ་མཐའ་ཡས་ཀྱང་།།
ཐོད་འཕྲེང་སྐྱེ་ལྔ་ཐུབ་དྲུག་རྒྱན་མཆོག་དང་།།
གྲུབ་ཆེན་བརྒྱད་ཅུ་སྤྲུལ་པའི་ཆོ་འཕྲུལ་སོགས།།
འགྲོ་བའི་དཔལ་དུ་གང་ལ་གང་འདུལ་ཤར།།

ཨོ་རྒྱན་ཡུལ་དུ་ཨིནྡྲ་བོ་དྷིའི་སྲས།།
དྷ་ན་ཀོ་ཤ་ར་མཚོ་སྐྱེས་རྡོ་རྗེ་འཆང་།།

རྒྱལ་སྲིད་བསྐྱུངས་ཤིང་འོད་འཆང་ཁབ་ཏུ་བཞེས།།
ཆོས་བཞིན་མཛད་པའི་རྒྱལ་པོ་ཐོར་ཅོག་ཅན།།

དུར་ཁྲོད་ཀུན་ཏུ་བརྟུལ་ཞུགས་སྤྱོད་པ་མཛད།།
མ་ཆོགས་དབང་བསྡུས་ཤཱནྟ་རཀྵི་ཏ།།

ཕག་མོའི་ཞལ་གཟིགས་གཟའ་ཀླུ་དམ་ལ་བཏགས།།
དངོས་གྲུབ་མཆོག་བརྙེས་རྡོ་རྗེ་དྲག་པོ་རྩལ།།

སློབ་དཔོན་ཆེན་པོ་པྲ་བྷ་ཧསྟི་ལས།།
རབ་ཏུ་བྱུང་བའི་ཤཱཀྱ་སེངྒེ་གསོལ།།

གསང་སྔགས་ཡོ་ག་ཕྱི་ནང་རིག་གནས་བཅས།།
ཐོས་བསམ་མཛད་དེ་བློ་ལྡན་མཆོག་སྲེད་རྩལ།།

མ་ར་ཏི་ཀར་ལྷ་ལྷུམ་མཛྷ་ར།།
ཕྱག་རྒྱར་བཞེས་ཚེ་འཆི་མེད་པདྨ་འབྱུང་།།

ཟ་ཧོར་རྒྱལ་ཁམས་འདུལ་དང་ཆོས་ལ་བཙུད།།
རྫུ་འཕྲུལ་མཆོག་གྲུབ་པདྨ་སཾ་བྷ་བ།།

ཡང་ལེ་ཤོད་དུ་ཡང་ཕུར་སྒྲུབ་མཛད་དེ།།
མཆོག་ཐུན་གྲུབ་པའི་རྡོ་རྗེ་ཐོད་ཕྲེང་རྩལ།།

བཀའ་འདུས་ཆོས་ཀྱིས་སྨིན་ཅིང་གྲོལ་བར་མཛད།།
མཆོག་གི་རིག་འཛིན་པདྨ་རྒྱལ་པོར་གྲགས།།

རྡོ་རྗེ་གདན་དུ་སྨུ་སྟེགས་རྩོལ་བ་བཟློག།

ཕྱོགས་ལས་རྣམ་རྒྱལ་སེངྒེ་སྒྲ་སྒྲོགས་རྩལ།།

སྟག་ཚང་སེང་གེར་བདུད་དང་དམ་སྲི་བཏུལ།།

འཚོལ་བའི་ཁྲོ་རྒྱལ་རྡོ་རྗེ་གྲོ་བོ་ལོད།།

ཞིང་ཀུན་དམ་ཆོས་འཕེལ་ཞིང་རྒྱས་པར་མཛད།།

སླར་ཡང་སྔོན་གྱི་ཐུགས་བསྐྱེད་དུས་བབས་ནས།།

ཟ་ཧོར་མཁན་པོའི་ལུང་གིས་སྐུལ་བ་ལྟར།།

ཆོས་རྒྱལ་ཚངས་པ་ལྷ་ཡི་མེ་ཏོག་གིས།།

སྤྱན་འདྲེན་ཕོ་ཉས་བསུ་བ་དང་བསྟུན་ནས།།

བོད་ཁམས་འདུལ་ཕྱིར་ཕེབས་པའི་ལམ་བར་དུ།།

བསྟན་མ་བཅུ་གཉིས་སྐྱོང་མ་བཅུ་གཉིས་དང་།།

མགུར་ལྷ་བཅུ་གསུམ་དགེ་བསྙེན་ཉེར་གཅིག་སོགས།།

སྣང་སྲིད་ལྷ་འདྲེ་ཐམས་ཅད་དམ་ལ་བཏགས།།
བོད་ཁམས་སྐྱོང་ཞིང་ཐུབ་བསྟན་སྲུང་མར་བསྐོས།།
གཞོང་པ་ལྷ་ཚུ་དོང་བའི་གདོང་ནས་བཏོན།།
རྫུ་འཕྲུལ་མི་ཡིས་རྒྱལ་བློན་ང་རྒྱལ་བཅགས།།

ཧས་པོ་རི་རྩེར་ཕྱུར་པའི་དཀྱིལ་འཁོར་བཞེངས།།
སླར་ཡང་ལྷ་འདྲེ་དམ་འདོགས་གཉིས་པ་མཛད།།
མཁའ་ལ་འཕྱུར་ནས་རྡོ་རྗེའི་འགྲོས་ཀྱིས་ནི།།
ས་གཞིར་བྱིན་རླབས་རྒྱལ་ཆེན་སྡེ་བཞི་སོགས།།

ལྷ་འདྲེ་ལས་བཀོལ་དཔལ་གྱི་བསམ་ཡས་བཞེངས།།
ཉིན་མོ་མི་དང་མཚན་མོ་ལྷ་འདྲེས་བཞེངས།།

ལོ་ལྔའི་བོངས་སུ་རྟེན་དང་བརྟེན་པར་བཅས།།
ངོ་མཚར་བཞོ་ཁྲིད་དུ་མས་འཕགས་པ་གྲུབ།།
སློབ་པཎ་རྣམས་དང་ལྷན་ཅིག་རབ་གནས་ཏེ།།
ནང་གི་ལྷ་རྣམས་ཕྱི་རུ་བྱོན་པ་དང་།།

ལྷོ་གླིང་རྫ་མཁྲིན་རྫ་སྙད་ལན་གསུམ་འཆོར།།
འཇའ་ཚོན་གཟུགས་དང་ཨ་རུའི་ཆར་ཆེན་བབས།།

རྩོལ་མོ་རང་འབྲོལ་ལ་སོགས་སྣ་ཚོགས་པའི།།
སྣ་ཚོགས་ཚོ་འཕྲུལ་བཀོད་པ་བསམ་ཡས་ཀྱིས།།
མི་དང་མི་མིན་སྐྱེ་དགུ་དྭངས་པར་བྱས།།
བྲག་དམར་ཀེའུ་ཚང་དཔལ་ཆེན་དབང་བསྒྱུར་ཏེ།།
བཀའ་བབས་ཐུགས་ཀྱི་བུ་དགུ་སྨིན་པར་མཛད།།

སོ་སོའི་ལུང་བསྟན་གནས་སུ་བསྒྲུབ་པ་ན།།
སྟན་ཐོག་གཅིག་ཏུ་གྲུབ་པའི་གོ་འཕང་གཤེགས།།
གཞན་ཡང་སློབ་ཚོགས་མཁའ་ལ་རྒྱུ་སྐར་བཞིན།།

ཆུ་བོ་རི་ཡི་སྒོམ་ཆེན་བརྒྱ་རྩ་དང་།།
འོད་ལུས་གྲུབ་པའི་མཁའ་འགྲོ་དུ་མས་མཚོན།།
གྲགས་པའི་མཚོ་ཆེན་བཞི་དང་ཕུག་ཆེན་བཞི།།
སྦས་གནས་རྒྱལ་པོ་བཞི་སོགས་རི་བྲག་ཀུན།།

སྒྲུབ་པའི་གནས་ཆེན་མཆོག་ཏུ་བྱིན་གྱིས་བརླབས།།
རི་སུལ་ཀུན་ཏུ་སྒྲུབ་པའི་སྡེ་ཡིས་ཁེངས།།
སྙིགས་འགྲོའི་དོན་དུ་ཟབ་གཏེར་མཐའ་ཡས་སྦས།།
སྤྲུལ་པས་གཏེར་ནས་འབྱིན་པར་ལུང་ཡང་བསྟན།།

བོད་ཀྱི་གདུལ་བྱ་མ་ལུས་མཛད་པའི་འཕྲོར།།
གུང་ཐང་ལ་ནས་ཅང་ཤེས་ཆིབས་དང་བཅས།།
འཛའ་ཚོན་ཕྲེང་ལས་ནམ་མཁར་འཕུར་ནས་ནི།།
འཛམ་གླིང་དོན་དུ་སྲིན་པོའི་ཁ་གནོན་ག་ཤེགས།།

ཚེ་བཅུ་ནམ་ཤར་ཉི་ཟེར་ལ་ཆིབས་ནས།།
བོད་ཁམས་སྐྱོང་བར་ཞལ་བཞེས་དབྱུགས་དབྱུང་འཚལ།།
གསོལ་འདེབས་བུ་ལ་འདུ་འབྲལ་མེད་དོ་ཞེས།།
ལྷ་སྲས་རྗེ་ལ་ནོར་བུ་དང་མཚུངས་པའི།།

ཞལ་ཆེམས་མན་ངག་བཅུ་གསུམ་བཅས་ཏེ་གནང་།།
མ་འོངས་ལུང་པ་རེ་ལ་གཏེར་སྟོན་རེ།།
ཡུལ་གྲུ་རེ་ལ་གྲུབ་མཆན་སྒྲོད་འཆང་རེ།།
གྲོང་སྡེ་རེ་ལ་མཆོད་གནས་དགེ་སློང་རེ།།

དེ་བཞིན་འདྲེ་འདུལ་ནུས་ལྡན་སྔགས་པ་རེ།།
བསྟན་འགྲོར་སྣན་མཛད་གང་ལ་གང་འདུལ་དུ།།
སྤྲུལ་པས་བོད་ཁམས་སྐྱོབས་པའི་ཞལ་བཞེས་དང་།།
ནམ་ཞིག་འགོང་པོས་བོད་ཁམས་འཕྱུང་དུས་སུ།།

བྲོས་ཡུལ་སྦས་གནས་ལམ་ཡིག་གསལ་པོར་སྟུལ།།
འཛམ་གླིང་སྤྱི་དང་ཁྱད་པར་གངས་ལྗོངས་ལ།།
རྒྱལ་བ་འདི་ལས་ལྷག་པའི་བཀའ་དྲིན་ཅན།།
གཞན་ན་མེད་དོ་བསམ་ཡོད་ཤེས་ལྡན་རྣམས།།

ཤེས་པར་ཁྲིས་ལ་གསོལ་བ་བརྒྱུན་དུ་ཐོབ།།
བསླུ་བ་མེད་པ་རྒྱལ་ཀུན་ཆོས་ཉིད་གཤིས།།
མཚོ་སྐྱེས་རྒྱལ་བ་འདི་ཡི་རིང་ལུགས་སྲོལ།།
འཛིན་པའི་རབ་སྔགས་སྔ་འགྱུར་རྙིང་མ་ཞེས།།

རིགས་ལ་གཟུར་གནས་རྣམ་དཔྱོད་ལྡན་ཡོད་ན།།
དད་པས་ཡིད་རབ་མི་འཕྲོགས་ཅང་སྲིད་དམ།།

དེ་ནི་བསྟན་པའི་ལྷག་མ་ཅུང་ཟད་འདིར།།
ཆགས་སྡང་མེད་པའི་དགེ་ལ་ཡིད་འཛགས་འཚལ།།
དེ་ཕྱིར་བདག་གཞན་དགེ་ལེགས་འདོད་པ་ཀུན།།
སྙིང་ནས་བག་ཟོན་མཛོད་ཅེས་ཐལ་མོ་སྦྱོར།།

རྣམ་ཐར་མདོར་བསྡུས་པད་དཀར་ཡིད་བཞིན་དབང་།།
ཆ་ཙམ་བརྗོད་འདིར་ཉེས་ཀུན་མཐོལ་ཞིང་འཆགས།།
རྣམ་དཀར་དད་པའི་ས་བོན་གང་མཆིས་པ།།
ཚོགས་གཉིས་ཡོངས་སུ་རྫོགས་པའི་རྒྱུར་གྱུར་ཅིག།

མགོན་པོ་འོད་དཔག་མེད་དང་སྤྱན་རས་གཟིགས།།
རྣམ་འཕྲུལ་གང་འདུལ་གུ་རུ་པདྨ་འབྱུང་།།
སྐུ་གསུམ་བླ་མ་དཀྱིལ་འཁོར་རྒྱ་མཚོའི་བདག།
རབ་འབྱམས་རྩ་གསུམ་འཁོར་ལོའི་བཀྲ་ཤིས་ཤོག།

མཁན་སློབ་ཆོས་རྒྱལ་ནམ་མཁའ་བཞིན་དུ་ཆེ།།
སངས་རྒྱས་བསྟན་པ་ལྷུན་པོ་བཞིན་དུ་བརྟེད།།
མདོ་སྔགས་བཤད་སྒྲུབ་ཉི་ཟླ་བཞིན་དུ་གསལ།།
བོད་ཀྱི་བདེ་སྐྱིད་དབྱར་མཚོ་བཞིན་དུ་རྒྱས།།

སྔ་ན་མེད་པའི་བཀྲ་ཤིས་དཔལ་འབར་བས།།
འཇིག་རྟེན་ཀུན་ཏུ་བདེ་ལེགས་འཕེལ་ཞིང་རྒྱས།།
ཆོས་སྲིད་ཕུན་ཚོགས་ནོར་བུའི་འོད་སྣང་གིས།།
བཀྲ་ཤིས་བདེ་ལེགས་ཕུན་སུམ་ཚོགས་པར་ཤོག།

གནས་མཆོད་རྡོ་རྗེ་གདན་དུ་སྟ་འགྱུར་གྱི།།
སྨོན་ལམ་ཆེན་མོའི་དྲན་དེབ་རྩོམ་སྒྲིག་པས།།
ཇི་ལྟར་བསྒྲུབ་པ་བཞིན་དུ་མདོར་བསྡུས་སུ།།
ཀུན་མིང་ཡི་ཤེས་རྡོ་རྗེས་བྲིས་ཏེ་ཕུལ།།
ངར་ཐང་སྒྲུལ་སྐྲུ་ཀུན་དགའ་དགེ་ལེགས།།

Namo Guru Bhye:
Homage to the Guru!
In the realm of Sukhāvatī, you are Protector Amitābha,
on Potala Mountain, Noble and Exalted Avalokiteśvara,
upon the Isle of Oḍḍiyāna, the Lotus Born One:
Lama inseparable from the Trikāya,
I bow in deep reverence before you.

Great Lotus Born Guru of Oḍḍiyāna!
If we tried to express a mere droplet of
the magnitude of the enlightened qualities you embody –
the 'Jam-dpal-sgyu-'phrul-drwa-ba,
the Magical Net of Mañjuśrī, says:
Glorious Lotus Born Buddha,
Omniscient Primordial Wisdom Treasure Holder,
Rāja Mayājāla King of Various Magic Feats,
Great One, Buddha Vidyāmantradhara.

And further:

Embodiment of the Enlightened Activity of
all the Buddhas of the Three Times,
you are the Incomparable Dharmakāya, Samantabhadra,
and the Sambhogakāya, Great Vajradhara.
Empowered with great compassion, appearing as Nirmāṇakāya,
your mighty enlightened activity tames all who need to be tamed,
and like a Wish-fulfilling Gem, you fulfill the wishes of all beings.

Our universe of a billion world systems, known as Patient Endurance, is the teaching domain of a single Supreme Nirmāṇakāya Buddha, and within it are one billion planet earths (Jambudvīpas).

The Bhagavan of this realm, Śākyamuni, principally turned the Dharma Wheel of the Vehicles of Exoteric Knowledge a billion times. Similarly, Guru Padmasambhava turned the Dharma Wheel of Esoteric Knowledge Beyond Conceptualization, the Secret Mantra Diamond Vehicle, a billion times. These pairs – Teacher and Teachings, Buddha and Padma, Exoteric and Esoteric – though different in appearance, are inseparable in the Dharmakāya, being the display of a single wisdom.

As it is said:
Samantabhadra abiding in the Dharmadhātu,
Great Vajradhara in the realm of Ghanavyūha,
and the Great Muni at the Vajrāsana are indivisible
and perfectly present as me, Padma.

And further:
I am known as Self Arisen Padma:
emerging from the Heart of Amitābha,
manifest from the Speech of Avalokiteśvara,
Lord of Compassion,
brother of all the Ḍākas, king of valiant heroes,
incomparable Ādibuddha Dharmakāya Samantabhadra,
and Great Sambhogakāya Vajradhara,
empowered with great compassion to appear as Nirmāṇakāya.

The Parinirvāṇa Sūtra says:
Now I am passing completely beyond all sorrow,
may all of you not create sorrow!
from the center of an immaculate, stainless lake
will arise one greater than I am.

From the dBus-'gyur-'chang-lung-bstan-pa'i-mdo-sde
(Sūtra of Predictions in Māgadha):
After I have disappeared,
when four years twice come to pass,
on the northwest border of Oḍḍiyāna,
on an island in Lake Dhanakośa
will arise a Noble One greater than the rest.

The Bla-med-don-rdzogs-'dus-pa'i-rgyud (Tantra of the
Perfect Embodiment of the Unexcelled Meaning) says:
After I have passed into Parinirvāṇa,
when two years short of a decade come to pass,
the most supreme Victor Over All the World,
known as the Lotus Born One of Oḍḍiyāna,
will be born from a lotus
to teach the Secret Mantrayāna; thus I prophesy.
So it is said here and in many other places.

And further:

The vast motivation of all the Buddhas of the ten directions
to benefit beings harmonized as a single intent,
and the unceasing continuum of
Kāya, Vaca, Citta, Guṇa, and Karma mandalas,
their entire essence gathered together into one,
dissolved into the heart of Buddha Amitābha,
as representative of the Dharmakāya.

The heart casket radiant with rainbow light
opened wide, and within a golden vajra marked with a HRĪ
shining with five-colored light appeared.

It alighted upon the broad pollen bed of a lotus
in the middle of the Sindhu Milky Lake of Dhanakośa
and dissolved into light.

And then the lotus blossom fully opened to disclose
Jñānakāya, luminous and perfected,
marked with all the auspicious signs of an enlightened being,
embodiment of primordial awareness instantaneously arisen,
overwhelmingly beautiful depths of shimmering light,
the most perfect Body, unstained by the womb,
the perfected form adorned with major and minor marks
of Buddhahood – Tsokyi Dorje, Lake-born Lotus Vajra!

At that moment, all the Buddhas of the Ten Directions
enthroned him and empowered him with their realization.
The entire assembly of Bodhisattvas and Sattmas, without exception,
dedicated themselves wholeheartedly to become allies and supporters
in his mission for the sake of benefiting beings.

The Ḍākas and Ḍākinīs of the three abodes were present,
eager to offer in unison their praise and encouragement.

Having been invited to take up the destiny of
being son of Indrabodhi, king of Oḍḍiyāna,
Padma was entrusted with royal dominion,
and for a while, that he manifested as the prince
ruling the land according to the Dharma.

But by numerous acts of skillful means,
Padma renounced the kingdom like so much spit in the dust.
Then in the presence of Guru Prabhahasti, Padma took ordination.

He accepted the saffron Dharma robes offered by the earth goddess.
The Buddhas of the ten directions arrived from the heavens
to empower him, saying, Wonderful, excellent! So be it!
And they honored him with the name Śākya Gelong Sumitra.

Then Padma proceeded to Arhat Ānanda, the attendant of
Bhagavat Śākyamuni. For five years, day and night continuously,
he played the role of studying the words and the meaning
of the entire range of the Causal Vehicle, the Lakṣaṇayāna.

Then Padma made a request of Ḍākinī Leykyi Wangmoche
for the complete inner, outer, and secret empowerments.
He completely mastered all of the Tantra Section (rgyud-sde)
of the Inner and Outer Mantrayāna.

From the Eight Great Accomplished Vidyādharas
such as Guru Mañjuśrīmitra and the rest, Padma
received the Sādhana Section (sgrub-sde)
of the Eight Heruka Teachings (bka'-brgyad).

Through the accomplishment of the maturation and liberation
practices connected with both the Tantra and Sādhana Sections,
signs of the great siddhis came forth.

At the Eight Great Cemeteries and other places,
in the company of mamos and Ḍākinī assemblies,
Padma sustained the fearless yogic disciplines of wisdom.

By means of inconceivable displays of Nirmāṇakāya emanations,
such as the Five Classes of Tod Treng (Garland of Skulls),
the Eight Manifestations of the Guru, the Six Munis,

Forty Emanations of Guru Padma, the Six Ornaments,
the Two Excellent Ones, the Eighty-Four Siddhas,
and through the Great Enlightened Action of completly
perfecting, comprehending, protecting, and spreading the
Sūtra and Mantra Teachings all across Ārya India
and throughout all universes,Padma caused the sun of
spiritual benefit and temporal happiness to rise.

From Tulku Garab Dorje and Rigdzin Śrī Siṃha and others,
Padma received the victorious summit of the Nine Yānas,
Man ngag Dzogpa Chenpo's Dharma Precepts,
deep and vast like an ocean, and he completely mastered them.

Moreover, in the western direction, in the land of Sahor, Padma
transformed a funeral pyre into a lake, with a lotus rising in the
center where he was seated upon its pollen bed in sacred union.
This and other incredible miraculous displays of various
and inconceivable kinds established those to be trained
in the abode of faith in an utterly compelling way.

Having introduced all beings to the Dharma,
Padma established them on the stage of Non-Returners.
Thus he is known as Padma Tod Treng Tsal,
Skull Garland Power.

Then in Tsub Gyur Tsal Rugged Grove
with the blessings of Vajra Vārāhī,
Padma bound under oath all the nāgas and planetary forces.

All the Ḍākas and Ḍākinīs of the Three Abodes
bestowed yogic powers upon Padma.

From this, he became known as Dorje Dragpo Tsal,
Powerful Vajra Wrath.

Then at Vajrāsana, when five hundred Tīrthika masters had instigated disputes, Padma rained down giant lightning bolts, liberating most of them and converting the rest to the teachings of the Buddha. Therefore he received the name Senge Dradrog, The Lion's Roar.

He beheld that the proper time and circumstances had arisen for the meeting of the Abbot, the Guru, and the King and the taming of the Land of Tibet. So in accord with the invitation issued by the emissaries and escort of the Jambudvīpa Dharma King Trisong Detsen, Padma proceeded gradually to Tibet, the Land of Snow.

Along the way, he bound under oath the Twelve Tenma goddesses, the Twelve Kyongma protectresses, the Thirteen Gurlha mountain spirits, Twenty-one Geynyen, and other nonhuman powerful ones, and appointed them as Dharma servants charged with protecting the Teachings.

His deeds of extracting a spring at Todlung known as Zhongpa Lhachu, Divine Water of the Basin, and taming the hubris of the king with magical fire from his five fingers illustrated his power. By the unlimited actions of a siddha, he tamed the beings to be tamed in Tibet.

The eight classes of gods and demons of all phenomenal existence Padma bound under oath and commanded. Samye Migyur Lungyi Drup's great temple,

together with the sacred statues it enshrined,
Padma completed entirely within the span of five years
through magical means.

During the consecration of the temple, the people's faith
swelled and instantly turned toward the Dharma.

Padma caused the great visionary gates of the inner sanctum
to open; the unchanging splendor of pure appearance welled
up and the torch of the Dharma blazed.

To transmit these lineages of light, Padma brought about
the maturation and liberation of Nine Heart Sons
and others, and then, in a single session, established
them on the lofty stage of Vidyādhara Siddha.
Assemblies of Tibetan disciples, human and nonhuman,
appeared like garlands of stars in the sky.

Because of Padma, retreat hermitages and meditation
centers covered the mountains and valleys of Tibet.
Padma blessed the Four Great Lakes of renown,
the Four Great Caves, the Four Kings of Hidden Lands,
and so forth, and all the remote mountain fastnesses
as places for Vidyādhara Siddhas.

With a magical display of emanations who could tame
anyone just as they required, he demonstrated
the great acts of a Buddha like this:

The deed of forming the intention to train beings,
the deed of entering into the lotus chamber,

the deed of self-arisen birth,
the deed of the prince's entertainment,
the deed of renunciation,
the deed of various austerities,
the deed of conquering the mārayas,
the deed of Buddha Enlightenment,
the deed of turning the Dharma Wheel,
the deed of fearless nondiscriminating yogic discipline,
the deed of concealing treasures,
so that the Dharma flourishes and does not decline.
So it is said.

And further:
All the Gu-ru'i-rnam-thar, the life stories of the Guru,
In the expanded or condensed versions, agree that
the most important actions are seeing and hearing
his enlightened biography with unbounded devotion and respect.
Through faith in this, one seizes the throne of liberation.
Have no doubt about attaining supreme Buddhahood.

Urgyan rNam-thar-mdor-bsdus-mdzad-pa,
Orgyan Lifestory Summary and Deeds, says:
Whoever writes or sees or hears or shows this text to others,
will be born in the Buddha-land of Sukhāvatī.
Through devotion and faith in this,
whoever acts in such a way harbors no doubts
about obtaining the highest enlightenment.
So it is said.

Ched-du brjod-pa'i-tshigs-su-bcad-pa,
Aphorisms in Verse, says:

When all the boundless Buddhas of the ten directions,
condensed their Kāya, Vaca, Citta, Guṇa, Karma into one,
and dissolved into Amitābha Buddha's Heart,
then that precious heart casket of rainbow light
opened wide. On the inside, the letter HRĪ of rainbow light
was radiantly shining.

In the northwestern land of Oḍḍiyāna,
in the center of the depths of the Spotless Lustrous Lake,
it would alight on top of a pollen bed of a self arisen lotus.

Without relying on the condition of having parents,
with auspicious marks and signs radiant, spontaneously perfected,
wondrous self arisen Rainbow Body Vajra Kāya
took birth in the manner of Wisdom freely rising.

All the Buddhas of the ten directions convened there,
bestowing empowerment with their pristine realization.
All the Bodhisattvas and Sattmas gathered, their pledges
to aid Him for the benefit of beings resounding.

Ḍākas and Ḍākinī Protectors of the Three Abodes
enthroned Him, singing praises and playing glorious music.
Throngs of virtuous protector gods and nāgas
bustled about, making clouds of offerings, inner, outer, and secret.

Just then, Orgyen Kandro Ling Chenmo's
Great Cakravartin Dharma King,
Most Excellent One renowned as Indrabhūti,
had come in search of jewels from the ocean.
Meeting Padma, Indrabhūti entreated him to be his son

and offered him the kingdom, which he ruled a while
according to Dharma.

Furthermore, Buddhas and Bodhisattvas of the ten directions
and assemblies of Ḍākas and Ḍākinīs of the Three Abodes,
exhorted Him with predictions to renounce the palace.
By performing many skillful actions, the kingdom
he did totally renounce, like so much spit in the dust.
In the presence of Prabhahasti he took ordination.

From Sayi Lhamo he received the saffron robe.
at that moment, the Buddhas gave their assent
declaring: "Well Done" and bestowed
the name Śākya Gelong Sumitra,
and another as well, Guru Śākya Senge.
This is Wangpo De, predicted by the Buddha.

Proceeding to Arhat Ānanda, the Muni's attendant,
Padma undertook the study of the Sūtras
for five years day and night continuously.

Having mastered the Lakṣaṇa Hetu Yāna,
he comprehended fully the words and meaning.
Then from Leykyi Wangmo the Foremost Ḍākinī
he received the outer, inner and secret empowerments
of the Mantrayāna.

At that time, after a mutual contest of minor magical powers
concluded with the proper conditions of
full faith and respect between master and disciple,
the Ḍākinī transformed Pad Jung into the syllable HUNG

and swallowed him. From her throat he transited the sacred body,
emerging through her secret lotus, thoroughly blessed.

Externally, she blessed him
as the embodiment of Buddha Amitābha:
He obtained the empowerments of Vidyādhara of Longevity.

Internally, she blessed him
as the embodiment of Most Excellent Avalokiteśvara:
He obtained the empowerments of Mahāmudrā meditation.

Secretly, she blessed him as the embodiment of Hayagrīva:
He obtained the empowerments of Binding Gods
and Demons under Oath.

An ocean of Vajrayāna (gsang-chen) Tantra Section (rgyud-sde)
maturation and liberation practices he received.
From Mañjuśrīmitra, Nāgārjunagarbha,
and the rest of the Eight Vidyādharas,
he requested the Sādhana Section (sgrub-sde) teachings.
From Rigdzin Śrī Siṃha and the others, (he received)
the teachings of Dzogpa Chenpo and resolved all doubts about it.

From Kukkurāja and a vast number of other masters,
he received the ripening and liberation practices
of oceans of the Secret Mantrayāna Tantras.

Having practiced, there was not one sign
of accomplishment that did not appear.
He practiced Amitāyus and accomplished
the deathless Vidyādhara state.

Endless displays of various magical manifestations –
the Five Tod Phreng, Six Munis, Six Ornaments,
and Two Most Excellent Ones, the Eighty Siddhas –
miraculous emanations arose for the welfare of beings,
training them in accordance with their needs.

In the Land of Oḍḍiyāna, you are Indrabhūti's son.
On Dhanakośa Lake, you are Tsokyi Dorje Chang.

You guided the kingdom, taking Prabhāvatī as your wife.
A king acting in accord with Dharma, you are Thorchog Chen.

Performing yogic practices in all the charnel grounds,
throngs of mamos submit to you, Śāntarakṣita.

Beholding the face of Vajra Vārāhī,
you bound planet spirits and nāgas under oath.
Obtaining the most excellent siddhi, you are Dorje Dragpo Tsal.
From Mahā Guru Prabhahasti you received ordination, Śākya Senge.

Mantrayāna Inner and Outer Yogas, and worldly knowledge as well,
you studied and contemplated, Loden Chogsed Tsal.

At Maratika with Princess Mandāravā as your consort,
you are Chimed Padma Jung, Immortal Lotus Born One.

To tame the Zahor kingdom and introduce the Dharma,
you created the supreme miraculous display, Padmasambhava.

At Yangle Shod you performed the Vajrakīlaya practices,
obtaining supreme and common siddhis, Dorje Tod Treng Tsal.

By means of Kadu (bka'-'dus) teachings,
maturation and liberation you accomplished,
most excellent Vidyādhara, renowned as Padma Gyalpo.

At Vajrāsana you defeated the Tirthika opponents,
victorious in All Directions, Senge Dradrog Tsal.

At Tagtsang Senge you tamed mārayas and evil forces,
crazy King of Wrath, you are Dorje Drolod.
Expanding Dharma in all realms and making it increase.

Moreover:
Since the time had come to fulfil the former Vow,
exhorted by the word's of the Abbot of Zahor,
Dharma King Tsangpa Lhayi Metog
sent envoys to invite and escort you.

And so in accord with that, to convert the land of Tibet,
you set forth, and, along the way,
the Twelve Tenma protectresses and
the Thirteen Gurla, the Twenty-one Geynyen –
all gods and demons you bound under oath and command
to be Protectors and Guardians of the Muni's Doctrine.

Zhongpa Divine Spring you opened
by penetrating the rock face with your staff.
With magic fire you humbled the pride of king and ministers.
On the peak of Hepori, you laid out the Kīla Mandala,
and bound the gods and demons a second time.
Flying in the sky, with the passage of your Vajra,
you consecrated the foundation, and the Four Guardian Kings,

gods, and demons you put to work for glorious Samye.
By day the humans toiled, by night, the gods and demons,

And in the space of five years, the sanctuary and its sacred forms,
wondrous art, distinctive and numerous, were completed.

When Gurus and Paṇḍitas together performed the consecration rites,
the gods of the temple interior came strolling outside.
In the Southern Isle Hayagrīva neighed three times.
Rainbow shapes and a great rain of medicinal aru fell.

Instruments played by themselves and all variety
of miracles took place. How inconceivable is Samye!
Humans, nonhumans, and all kinds of beings felt elevated
and full of faith.

At Dragmar Keutsang you bestowed the Palchenpo empowerment.
Holders of the transmission lineage, the Nine Heart Sons,
you matured and gave each a prediction:
If they were to practice at a certain place,
then in a single session,
they would traverse to the stage of Siddha

And more:
Throngs of disciples you had, as many as stars in the sky,
including, at Chubori the hundred hermits
and illustrated by the many Ḍākinīs
who accomplished the rainbow body.

The famous Four Great Lakes and Four Great Caves,
the Four Kings of Hidden Lands, mountain and rocky retreats all,

you blessed as excellent and sacred places to practice.
Every hill and vale was covered with Dharma hermitages.

To benefit beings in this degenerate age,
boundless treasures you concealed,
then predicted their discovery by emanated ones.

At the conclusion of your deeds for the beings to be trained in Tibet,
at Gung Thang Pass mounted on the all-knowing horse,
riding a rainbow, you flew up into the sky,
departing to subdue the demons for the sake of the world.

When the tenth day comes, mounted on the rays of the sun
you come to protect Tibet, your promise guarantees.
For your children who pray to you,
there is no meeting and parting, you say.

On Prince Lhasrey you bestowed your final testament
and thirteen upadeśa, precious like jewels.

For the future, for each valley, a Terton you predicted;
for each district, the names of those guarding the conduct,
and for each village, the priests and the monks.

In the same way each demon tamer, powerful Mantrin.
For the sake of the Dharma and for beings,
to bring benefit in whatever ways are needed,
through your emanations, you have promised to protect Tibet.

And eventually, when the time comes that evil forces
bring ruin on Tibet,

you will bestow clearly the guide books
to the hidden sanctuaries and places of refuge.

For the world in general and the Land of Snow in particular
there is no other Buddha more merciful than you.
Thus the wise ones, who have reflected, come to trust.
They always obtain their requests for what needs to be known.

Non-deceiving Dharmatā nature of all the Buddhas,
Tsokyi Gyalwa, this Lotus Buddha's tradition—
its upholders are known as Supreme Mantrayāna
Ngagyur Nyingma, Ancient Ones.

An impartial witness, a discerning one
who barely scratched the surface of this tradition
would have to wonder: is it even possible
for the heart not to be enthralled by faith?

Today when only a fragment of Dharma remains in the world,
the virtue of being free from desire and hatred
is where mind should settle.

May we wish only for goodness and virtue
For ourselves and others, with all our hearts.
Hands folded together, I entreat you: Take good care.

The abbreviated life story of the White Lotus, Wish-fulfilling King.
As for this little piece expressed here,
all its faults, I admit and confess.
Whatever seeds of pure faith are found therein,
may they become the cause for completing the two accumulations.

Protector Amitābha and Avalokiteśvara,
magical incarnation, Great Taming Guru Padma Jung,
Trikāya Lama, who embodies oceans of mandalas, to you we pray.
May there always be the good fortune
of the mandala of the immeasurable Three Roots,
the Guru, Deva, and Ḍākinī!

May the tradition of the Abbot, Guru, and King
be great as the sky.
May the teachings of the Buddha
blaze magnificent, like Mount Meru.
May the Sūtra and Mantra exposition and practice traditions
shine like the sun and moon.

May the happiness and well-being of Tibet expand like a summer lake.
May unprecedented good fortune be ours, and forever increase,
fostering happiness and virtue, abundant, for the whole world.
May both the Dharma and the secular world flourish,
and through the shining light of these jewels,
may every excellence and fortune come!

Composed upon request for the Memorial Annals of the
Ngagyur Monlam Chenmo held at the most holy site of Bodh Gayā,
written as a brief summary by Yeshe Dorje and offered to you.

PADMASAMBHAVA

Padmasambhava Comes to Tibet

PADMASAMBHAVA

Introduction

Padmasambhava, the renowned saint and scholar of the eighth century, became a central figure in the shaping of Buddhism's history in Tibet. Born from the lotus of compassion and revered as the 'second Buddha', he entered this world to enlighten all beings. As his biography relates, Guru Padmasambhava is the manifestation of the compassion of the Bodhisattva Avalokiteśvara, the speech of Amitābha, and the body of Śākyamuni Buddha. All the Buddhas of the Ten Directions and the Three Times of past, present, and future are identical in essence and collectively embodied in the Great Guru. Just as the Buddha's teaching is the same for all but is interpreted variously by those on different stages of the spiritual path, so Padmasambhava appears in different ways according to the receptivity of those seeking liberation.

This account of Padmasambhava's life operates on many levels. While his origins and various episodes in his career are shrouded in mystery, we know that he appeared on this earth as a great seeker and integrator of the Vajrayāna teachings. In worldly matters, such as language, logic, the earth sciences, the fine arts, and even architecture, Padmasambhava was the quintessence of a true 'renaissance man'. In his travels, he exhaustively sought out and mastered the teachings of human and non-human guides, practiced austerities to subdue the demons of cupidity-attachment, aversion-hatred, and bewilderment-erring, and received numerous initiations. At the time of his invitation to Tibet, he was renowned as the foremost scholar and tantric master at the University of Nālandā. Upon his arrival in Tibet, he did not entertain obstacles, but instantly transmuted countless manifestations of negativity. In a short time, he had safeguarded the tantric teachings in the hearts and minds of the Tibetan people.

In the grandeur of the mountain highlands, Padmasambhava encountered numerous capricious spirits, personifications of the emotional undercurrents of the entire Tibetan civilization. At once he was faced with the prevailing powers of primitive mythic beliefs, hostile natural forces, and wrathful wielders of destructive magic. His first task, therefore, was to provide new explanations for ancient understandings and to demonstrate, in a skillful and unsullied manner, the deepest and most mystic aspects of human existence. He could not ignore the pre-existing Tibetan predilection for magic and the world of spirits, for Buddhism has always recognized that demonic or godlike forms are the expression of our own minds. To subdue wrathful spirits is to tame our own emotionality and thus to dispel serious obstacles to our spiritual growth.

While the miraculous acts performed by the Great Guru may appear to some to be an ostentatious display of his psychic accomplishments, his deeds were inspired by a higher purpose. By encountering these malevolent demons, he not only transformed their hostile displays into an energetic appreciation for the Dharma, he also entrusted to their charge the responsibility of protecting and safeguarding the sacred teachings. Similarly, his words and deeds convinced Tibetans that they would remain helpless against the demons inflicting wrath upon their country until they sought the truth in their own minds. While this realization sent a shaft of fear into their hearts, his acts also encouraged them with hope, for they provided the king and his subjects the basis for awakening confidence in him and in the Dharma. In this way he prepared them to receive the liberating teachings of the Tantras.

As the dispeller of darkness and the immediate expression of Buddhahood, Guru Rinpoche addresses himself to the consciousness of all beings. More implicitly, episodes in Padmasambhava's biography express meditation experiences in terms of events in the outer world. To some, for example, he may appear in wrathful form as Dorje Drolod, fearlessly treading underfoot the ever-deceptive ego and severing karmic entanglements by wielding his three-edged dagger (phur-bu). To others he appears as the central figure of a radiant mandala, an all-discerning friend, refuge, and inner guide. By subduing the self-created demons and fascinations of our individual predispositions, Guru Rinpoche lays bare the apparitional nature of selfish aims and exposes the mind as utterly pure and ready to receive any content without bias. He challenges every manifestation of negativity with an attitude that each situation in life, regardless of its outward appearance, can prove to be an instruction in truth.

If, in the course of Guru Rinpoche's biography, certain episodes seem ambiguous or are couched in metaphorical language, it is because the essential meaning is revealed in silence, beneath the level of specific terms and concepts. One is left to measure and test the authenticity of psychological insights from within meditation.

On the innermost level, Padmasambhava is not intended to be viewed as a mere historical figure having a psychosomatic constitution just like ours, for he is no ordinary being. Like a rainbow, he is pure, transparent, untouchable, and clear. He is all-knowing and all-beautiful: The Buddhas of the Three Times shine from the pores of his skin. His entire form is pure light in a world of absolute perfection. He sits on a lotus seat of compassion and a sun throne of highest wisdom, which reside in the heart of the meditator. From here, the illuminated mind of the Guru fills the ten directions of space like the rays of the sun. He is the embodiment of the Three Kāyas (Trikāya): his view is the all-embracing, absolute awareness (Dharmakāya); his thoughts are in perfect attunement with every situation (Sambhogakāya), and all his actions are the on-going expression of the very nature of the universe (Nirmānakāya). Timeless, ageless, and deathless, unoriginated, not dependent on externals, and untainted by suffering, he manifests through a variety of forms which he assumes at various times – and in this time – to teach the Diamond Path.

Constant and mindful meditation on the pure essence of the Guru destroys all selfish desires, inappropriate qualities, and unnecessary delusions, so that one learns to view every situation as the means to attain Buddhahood in this lifetime. Ordinarily, the mind is diffused and wandering, but when this meditation is property enacted, every form one sees becomes the body of Padmasambhava, every sound one hears becomes the speech of Padmasambhava, and each action becomes an expression of the Great Guru's mind.

PADMASAMBHAVA

TSOKYI DORJE

Birth of the Lotus-Born Guru

In the land of Uḍḍiyāna[1] lived the blind king Indrabhūti, a wealthy and compassionate ruler who in times past had freely given his wealth and even his eyesight for the welfare of his people. Upon the death of his only son and heir, Indrabhūti was overwhelmed with sorrow, for famine and drought afflicted the land, the royal treasury was exhausted, and the people were reduced to eating unripened grain and flowers. Making offerings of all their possessions, the king and his people prayed to the immortal Buddhas.

Their prayers were heard by the Great Bodhisattva Avalokiteśvara. Looking down from the Sukhāvatī heaven, the All-seeing Lord appealed to Amitābha, the radiant Buddha presiding over that western paradise, to bestow upon these suffering beings the blessings of enlightened compassion. Immediately from Amitābha's tongue there went forth a ray of red light that blazed through the sky like a meteor and entered the center of Lake Dhanakośa. On the spot where the light had entered, a lotus blossom spontaneously unfolded. As the great flower opened, Amitābha emitted from his heart the mantric syllable HRĪ, which fell in the shape of a golden dorje into the center of the lotus. There, in a mist of rainbow light and surrounded by Ḍākinīs, sat the essence of all Buddhas in the appearance of an eight-year-old boy. Thus sent forth from the heart of Amitābha, the supremely compassionate Buddha, the Lotus-born Guru appeared in the world to aid all beings.

Indrabhūti, meanwhile, downcast and near despair, resolved to risk his life for the good of his people. Setting out on a hazardous journey, he sought to obtain a wondrous wish-fulfilling gem from the nāgas who dwelt beneath the waters of the ocean. When he arrived, the nāgas greeted him with offerings of precious stones, and the Goddess of Azure unveiled a brilliant blue gem. With this auspicious gem safely concealed in his garments, the king uttered a wish, and his blind left eye was immediately restored to sight.

Returning from the palace of the nāgas, the king beheld a five-colored rainbow arching over Lake Dhanakośa. Looking more closely, he discovered the young boy sitting on the pollen bed of an enormous lotus, his body shining like the sun. Believing this shimmering sight to be a dream, the king asked the child who he was and from whence he came. The boy replied, "I have no parents, but am born spiritually, the gift of Amitābha and Avalokiteśvara. As foretold by the Buddha, I have come to aid all beings and reveal the doctrine of the Inner Mantras." Hearing this, the king completely recovered his sight and joyfully enthroned the youth as his son and heir, naming him Padma Jungnay (Lotus-born). Thereafter, in the land of Uḍḍiyāna, vapor arose from the sea, clouds formed in the sky, rain fell, flowers blossomed, and fruits ripened. With this, depression and fear lifted from the hearts of the people.

When the Lotus-born prince grew to maturity, Indrabhūti, who had now grown old, arranged his marriage to a beautiful princess from Siṃhala. Anointing the young prince his successor as king of Uḍḍiyāna, Indrabhūti named him Padma Gyalpo (Lotus King). In secret, the old king presented Padma with the wish-fulfilling gem, saying, "This will satisfy all your desires." But the prince returned it replying, "Whatever I behold is my wish-fulfilling gem." Then, requesting King Indrabhūti to extend his opened hand, the prince instantaneously produced another gem.

Padma's attainment of the heights of worldly power and sensuous enjoyment soon led to the realization that possessions, wealth, and prestige are ultimately illusory, transitory, and unsatisfying. Recalling the great renunciation of the Buddha, he decided to renounce his home and kingship, saying, "This worldly life is transitory, the activities of saṃsāra are endless, and separation is inevitable. Since this is the law of the world, I will fix my thoughts on attaining liberation." Soon, however, it happened that Padma was held karmically responsible for killing the wife and demon son of a minister. Banished into exile, he took up the life of a yogi.

Seeking the Teachings

Wandering among the eight famous cemeteries (cremation grounds) of India, Padma practiced meditation without distraction. Then he proceeded to the Cool Sandalwood cemetery near Bodh Gayā.

Using corpses for his seat, he entered into deep samādhi and continued meditation for five years. Peaceful Ḍākinīs often visited him and gave him empowerments and oral instructions. For food he took the offerings made to the dead, and for clothing, he used the shrouds of the corpses. In each of the eight cemeteries he received ritual practices (sādhana) from the guardian Herukas (wrathful male deities) and siddha masters (accomplished yogis), who hold the secrets of enlightenment. While meditating for numerous years in these cemeteries, Padma traveled through space to different realms and world-systems, requesting instructions in the esoteric teachings. Through constant practice he acquired mastery over all the restless and destructive forces of nature. For this accomplishment he became known as Dorje Dragpo, the Indomitable Wrathful One.

URGYAN DORJE CHANG

Then Padma walked to Bodh Gayā. Multiplying his body so that it appeared like a vast multitude of yogis, he astounded the crowd of onlookers, who asked who he was and what guru he followed. Padma replied, "I have no guru, but am the Self-born Buddha." Still, seeing that these people and those of future generations would need spiritual guidance, Padma disciplined himself in the three yogas of body, speech, and mind and continued to study with teachers in both human and non-human realms. In order to guide others, he desired to find a doctrine capable of being explained in a few words, which, when applied, would prove immediately effective, just as the sun, once it has risen, immediately gives heat and light.

Journeying to the country of Padmāvatī, Padma mastered the art of healing, learning diagnoses and an innumerable variety of remedies. In the land of Ragala, Padma met an old white-haired man known as Friend of All, and asked him, "Old man, what is your knowledge?" The old man replied, "In teaching language and writing, I have no rival in the world beneath the sun." "Then," Padma said, "kindly teach me language and writing." Then, from Friend of All, Padma learned Sanskrit, the language of the gods, and many other dialects – 360 languages and sixty-four forms of writing in all. Thereafter, he mastered the arts of the lapidary and the potter and became skillful in all crafts. In this way Padma proceeded, receiving whatever instruction he requested.

From Ānanda he received an account of all the Sūtras and commentaries that had been recorded in writing. From Buddhaguhya he received the Mahāyoga Tantras, from Śrī Siṃha the Tantras of the Supreme Heruka, and from Garab Dorje the Atiyoga teachings, the most sublime of the Tantras. Visited by Bodhisattvas from other realms, Padma learned all that was known concerning astrology, philosophy, logic, physics, and the combined wisdom of all other worlds. His next teacher was an ordained Ḍākinī who manifested before him one hundred peaceful and wrathful deities and transformed him into the syllable HŪM. Then she initiated him into the Hayagrīva mandala, empowering him to overcome all conflicting spiritual beings and mental forces.

Thus, having practiced the outer, inner, and secret traditions of the Tripiṭaka, and having received the precepts, explanations, initiations, and empowerments of the Tantras, Padma became a complete master of all existing knowledge. Before him who was the mind-incarnation of the Buddha Amitābha there spontaneously appeared the mandala of the Unity of All Buddhas and Bodhisattvas. Externally he appeared as a brown-robed monk, but inwardly he was master of the supreme secret mantras.

Then Padma attained the yogic arts of clairvoyant seeing, hearing, feeling, smelling, and tasting by practicing austerities which assisted his development of breath control and the resultant 'psychic ear'. Having acquired knowledge as limitless as the sky, he journeyed to the cemetery where dwelled the tantric deity, Mahākāla. There, resting his back against a stūpa adorned with precious gems, he taught the Mahāyāna and Vajrayāna teachings to the Ḍākinīs. He who had traveled far and wide was called in India Nyima Odzer, Ray of the Sun, and in Nepal became known as Loden Chogsed, Transmitter of Wisdom to all Worlds.

Padmasambhava Travels throughout the World

Padmasambhava then journeyed to the land of Zahor where he preached the Dharma and gave instructions in the Mantrayāna to the king's daughter, Princess Mandāravā. However, the people became scandalized, believing that a monk was cohabiting with a woman, and reported this to the king. The king became enraged, confined his daughter to a pit of thorns, and condemned the Guru to be burned alive. But the Lotus-born Teacher, in full command of all natural forces, transformed his cremation pyre into an immense lake surrounded by a burning ditch. In the center of this lake, an ivory-petalled lotus supported a child of eight, whose translucent body glowed with the purplish color of seashells. The king, rubbing his eyes, saw the child encircled with haloes of multicolored lights that illuminated the entire great arch of the sky. Repenting his error, he offered his throne to the Guru, naming him Padmasambhava, Born from a Lotus.

ŚĀKYA SENGE

Then Amitāyus, Buddha of Boundless Life, came in a vision to Padmasambhava and Mandāravā as they were meditating in a cave. Placing the urn of immortality on their heads, he rendered their bodies luminous and henceforth immune to illness, old age, and death. Thereupon Padmasambhava constructed the mandalas of the wrathful deities and demonstrated the effective methods of doctrine and conduct, whereby one may, step by step, attain nirvāṇa.

Stainless as a diamond, the Guru then returned to his birthplace, Uḍḍiyāna, and appeared in public with his woman disciple, asking for alms. But the royal ministers recognized him saying, "This is the former prince who abandoned his wife and then murdered the minister's son. What catastrophe will he now bring upon the country? He aspires not to good, but to crime." With all the ministers in agreement, they commanded that loads of sandalwood and measures of oil be brought and commited the couple to the flames. When the smoke from the pyre failed to disperse after twenty-one days, the king together with all his ministers visited the site. There they beheld an enormous lake, where the couple, entwined and haloed in rainbow auras, danced in the center of a full-blown lotus. Humbly, the king of Uḍḍiyāna asked for blessings and teachings. Padmasambhava replied, "The three worlds are like a prison house. Even though you are a wise king and possess every material comfort, you cannot escape the material and sensual attachments that cause you frustration and mental suffering. But knowledge of temporal impermanence and the inevitability of death will guide you to honor this precious life, abandon worldly illusions, and teach you to govern your mind." Thus saying, Padmasambhava became known as Dorje Drolod, The Eternal Comforter of All Beings. He stayed in Uḍḍiyāna for thirteen years, instructing the populace in the outer, inner, and secret mantric formulas. Many inhabitants of that land became successful practitioners and passed away in a brilliant rainbow light, leaving behind no physical trace.

Padmasambhava traveled widely in India and Nepal, giving instructions in the Mantrayāna. He also journeyed throughout this world, passing through South India and Śrī Lankā, Indonesia, and

Burma; through Central Asia and parts of China and Russia; through Afghanistan, Persia, Egypt, and Africa; to Shambhala, Sumeru, and other mystic lands, and to other realms as well. In all these lands he subdued fierce mountain gods, barbaric cannibal spirits, and demons of pestilence and plague. To all dark planetary forces he brought the harmonious influence of the Dharma, and for those tormented by mental anguish, emotional instability, and lack of confidence, he dispelled the causes and manifestations of bewilderment, dissatisfaction, frustration, and other forms of negativity, and demonstrated the blessings of cultivating equanimity.

In Southeast Asia, in Zangling, Land of Copper, a tīrthika (non-Buddhist) king had Padmasambhava bound and thrown into the river. But the Guru burst his bonds and flew up into the sky, where he danced in the air. Amazed, the ruler and his people abandoned their fierce ways and converted to the Dharma. From this demonstration, Padmasambhava became known as Vajra Garuḍa, 'Diamond Bird', the Indestructable Lord of the Skies. When another tīrthika king poisoned him to prevent him from teaching the Dharma, the Precious Guru transmuted the poison in his body into pure and radiant light.

Once, when the scholars of Nālandā Mahāvihāra, the renowned Buddhist university, were being challenged in philosophical debate by powerful proponents of opposing doctrines, they said among themselves, "Although we can defeat them in philosophy, we cannot overcome their occult powers." Thus, making many prayers and offerings, the Buddhists invited Padmasambhava. The next morning at dawn, the Guru arrived at the palace and descended through the branches of trees like a great bird. Seated in meditation, he emanated four personalities resembling his own. Challenging his opponents' dualistic arguments, he convinced the non-Buddhists to doubt their own views. In the next competition, when the non-Buddhists magically produced leaping flames of fire, Padmasambhava touched the earth, and a great lotus blossom sprang forth. A wide swash of sun-bright flame leaped from the pollen bed, rising beyond sight into the sky. Quelling by these means all doubts concerning the power of the Buddhadharma, the Guru became known as Senge Dradog, Lion-Master of Wisdom.

Padmasambhava also traveled to Nepal, where earthquakes, storms, floods, and other natural disasters were devastating the land, destroying both animals and harvests. While meditating in the grotto of Yanglayshod, he assumed the wrathful form of Vajrakīla (Dorje Phurbu). Through the intensity of his concentration, he subdued eight different classes of conflicting and disruptive beings, which then vowed to protect and defend the Dharma in Nepal. Through these and other actions, Padmasambhava transmuted the obscuring powers of bewilderment into a stream of peaceful existence and exemplified the unerring integrity and compassion of all Buddhas.

The Advice of the Bodhisattva Abbot

The work of perfecting mankind is guided by the three Bodhisattvas known as the Lords of the Three Families: Mañjuśrī, Lord of Wisdom; Avalokiteśvara, Lord of Compassion; and Vajrapāṇi, Lord of Mystic Power. In order to bring the Dharma to the plateaus of

Tibet, they appeared as three early kings of that land. Avalokiteśvara manifested as Songtsen Gampo, the first Buddhist king of Tibet, whose two queens, a Chinese and a Nepalese princess, were emanations of merciful female Bodhisattvas. Mañjuśrī appeared as King Trisong Detsen, and Vajrapāṇi as King Ralpachen.

Trisong Detsen, eager to spread the Buddhadharma in his kingdom, invited from India the learned scholar and gentle Bodhisattva Śāntarakṣita, and placed the construction of the Self-created Temple of Samye under his direction. One auspicious morning, the king, robed in white silk, took a golden pickaxe smeared with unguents and dug to the depth of one cubit, whereupon three oils oozed up from the earth, one red, one yellow, and one white. Spreading these oils over his face and anointing his head, the king proclaimed, with great joy, the coming of the Buddha's Doctrine to the Land of Snows. Thus were the foundations laid for the building of Samye monastery.

Padmasambhava Comes to Tibet

The priests and shamans of the Bonpo religion, however, did not wish to relinquish either their governing social status or their cultural heritage. Resisting the intrusion of new and different teachings, they called upon wrathful beings for help. These beings, manifestations of powerful natural forces, began to destroy by night what men had built during the day, restoring all the earth and stones to their original places. Realizing that social insurrection and chaos would ensue if Śāntarakṣita remained, Trisong Detsen reluctantly requested him to depart. But the Abbot replied, "I have endeavored to perfect the spirit of a Bodhisattva. If gentleness cannot prevail, we must rely upon one who is learned in the five classes of knowledge and before whom all negative forces tremble and become powerless. At this very moment, Padmasambhava, the Doctor from Uḍḍiyāna, resides near the Diamond Throne of India. All your hopes for the people of Tibet will materialize if you invite this incarnate Buddha of the Three Times."

Padmasambhava Is Invited to Tibet[9]

Siddharāja, after traveling in India,
came to King Trisong Detsen with this news:
"In the Indian land the crowd of pandits
is like the crowd of stars, without number.
The one who among them all has demonstrated himself the highest
is Guru Padmasambhava,
who presides in the cavern in the Lofty Schist Mountains.
He was not born from a womb, but by apparition;
he is a renowned incarnation."
The king was moved to great joy by these words
and he dispatched three messengers:
Trisher, also called Dorje Dudjom, of the village of Ba,
Śākyaprabha of the Chims clan,
and the military count Palgyi Senge.
To all four he sent gold dust and golden bowls

PADMASAMBHAVA

to be borne to the Diamond Throne of India.
The four lotsawas crossed the Indian plain.
To King Sūrya they presented a measure of gold dust,
a golden bowl and a message;
to the great ceremonial pandit, one measure;
to Padma of Uḍḍiyāna, one measure and a golden bowl.
The Great Guru graciously received the royal gifts.
Then the envoys spoke: "The King of Tibet Trisong Detsen
has decided to found a seat for the faith, a monastery of meditation,
but the spirits are obstructing him.
We invite you to consecrate the blessed soil,
and to secure, preserve, and defend the Buddha's Doctrine;
we beseech you to show yourself well disposed."
The Great Saint of Uḍḍiyāna having agreed to this request,
in the earth male tiger year,
on the fifteenth day of the winter midmoon,
under the sign of the Pleiades, set out on his way.
By new moon they had reached Nepal.
Then Padma, the Doctor of Uḍḍiyāna, said to them:
"I am going to wrestle with the genies of Tibet and to subdue the land;
I will be there before long;
until then the spirits born sexually must hold their peace.
You, the lotsawas, go on ahead!"
And he dispatched them in advance,
giving them his protective blessing.

The Great Saint of Uḍḍiyāna spent three lunar months in Nepal.
After granting great benefactions on the Nepalese Vasudhara
and many others in Nepal,
he hid a treasure in the monastery of Ekāra.
Then, in the grotto of Yang Leshod,
in that of Asura and other grottoes,
in the monastery of Shankhu and other Nepalese monasteries,
at the crag called Mighty Soil, and other places round about,
he hid a thousand other treasures.

Then, on the first day of the first summer month,
when he had decided to go on and had started his journey,
the trees of India and Nepal pointed their crests toward Tibet,
and all the flowers facing Tibet blossomed.
The pandits of India and Nepal had dreams with bad omens:
that the sun and moon rose together in Tibet,
that all the law of India transferred in its entirety to Tibet,
and that the barbarian region was bedecked with monasteries.
At this, the ḍākinīs of all four orders cried out graspingly:
"The Guru is leaving for Tibet. Postpone such a declaration!
Diamond Master, Treasure of Thought,
what is your reason to teach the treetops?
Why are the flowers blossoming?
The pandits' nightmares, have they a reason?
It is wrong for the Glorious Mandala to recede;
for the Guru to leave is as though
the unshakable unmoving sky were leaving.
The Spontaneous Infinity of the Four Elements,
the Guru, is leaving; he will not stay.
Infinite Spontaneous Benefaction for Beings,
we beg the Guru not to depart, but to remain."
Thus they spoke. The Master answered,
"Oh, conspiring ḍākinīs, listen to me!

"At the beginning of the summer season, fruits swell with juice;
besought by those in need of conversion, pity springs up.
Having seen the law of karma, I do not have the time to linger;
the garuḍa is soaring – his wings outspread.
For me, benefits and happiness are sunk in the past,
and the time has come for the impartial benefiting of others.
Mother and sister ḍākinīs, may the Dharma befriend you!"

Having spoken thus, the Guru arrived at Mang Yul.
There, in the presence of the Nepalese woman Śākyadevī,
he predicted:

"After the lapse of more than two hundred generations,
in the districts Purang and Mang Yul of the Three Appanages,
a king, Gonsum, will arise from among your descendants.
In Kashmir, three noble brothers from Turkestan will be famous.
In Nepal, from the interior of the Ekāra monastery,
the hidden Holy Law of Uḍḍiyāna will be made manifest.
In the town of Langlar, the monastery Pelgay will appear.
If poor folk lay down body and life for the Dharma,
their axis of faith will prove to be a substantial pillar."
He spoke, and Śākyadevī, the Nepalese woman,
placed her trust in the Master Who Will Mold the World.

Now, clairvoyantly, the Great One from Uḍḍiyāna deemed
that the time had come to effect conversion through the forces
of deeds, and he went to Lake Nyimakhud in Nepal.
Seven royal envoys met him there, to entreat him
once again to enter Tibet. Namkhay Nyingpo headed
the delegation, accompanied by the chief of Bay Mang,
Nangseng Gong Lhalung, a man from Dab, Kruzing,
one from Chogro, Belsung Gon, Duddul of the Nanam clan,
then Putrasri of Sha, and finally the minister Tagna Dongsig.

They all wondered at Padmasambhava:
"He has overcome Mang Yul. How was that possible?
His investigation embraces everything; he scrutinizes essential truth.
He brings about the festival of increasing joy by means of the Dharma;
through his fortune-binding benediction he plants hope
within one's mind. It is thanks to him
that faith arises in the Holy Dharma."

Conversing thus, and carrying the inscribed roll and the gold dust,
they reached their destination.
At this side of Nepal, facing India,
they met the One of Uḍḍiyāna, Padmasambhava,
and handed him the inscribed roll together with the king's presents.
Thereupon, the Guru sent these seven intercessors
ahead of him to Samye.

The Great One from Uḍḍiyāna, after mounting to the sky,
remained in the central plain of Mang Yul for three lunar months.
In high places and low, in caves and crevasses he hid a treasure.

Trisong Detsen, King of Tibet, forthwith dispatched Kawa Paltseg,
Dorje Dudjom, and Chogrolui Gyaltsen bearing gold;
on their way they talked day and night, wearing themselves out.
And when the Guru's ḍākinī-guardians invited them to express
a wish, the three couriers, overwhelmed with fatigue,
begged that they should be conveyed as far as
Mang Yul's central plain.

PADMA GYALPO

After admitting them to an audience, the Master asked
though he already knew: "Who are you?"
"We are Tibetans, come with an invitation for the Guru", they said
as they bowed down to him and offered him a measure of gold dust.
"Are these presents from the ruler of the Town of the Deceased?"
Thus saying, he threw the gold to the farthest limits of Mang Yul and
Nepal. But he saw that the loss affected them painfully, and said,
"Hold out the flaps of your cloaks!"
And he filled them with earth and pebbles.
When, one by one, they opened the flaps and looked,
all was gold, silver, turquoises, and precious stones.
Filled with complete confidence,
they conceived great respect for the Saint.

Padmasambhava Subdues the Demons of Tibet

Then, in the autumn, Padma came to the castle of Mang Yul.
A Fury of the region of Zhang Zhung, Jamun the Eminent Enemy,
thought she could crush the Guru between two stone mountains.
But he rose up in the sky, and the humiliated Fury
offered the heart of her life.
As her secret name she was called Debt of Turquoises and Diamonds,
and the Guru gave her a great treasure to watch over.

Then, on the Plateau of the Sky, he reached the Black Castle.
The white ḍākinī of the glaciers thought
a thunderbolt would destroy him,
but the Guru, surrounding her with one finger,
swept her away into a lake.
The terrified ḍākinī fled as far as the lake of Palmo Paltang.
At once the water began to boil, the flesh dropped from her bones,
and the Guru, hurling a vajra, blinded her in one eye.
Whereupon she rose above the surface and uttered this supplication:

"Face of the Master! Oh, Vajra! Dorje Todtreng Tsal!
I swear I will do no more harm. This solemn promise comforts me.
What else can I do? I yield; I approach as the Guru's vassal."
And she gave the heart of her life, while he bound her by an oath.
As her secret name she was called the Unfleshed Turquoise
and Diamond Lamp,
and he committed a great treasure to her care.

Then he came to Oyug Bremo,
where the twelve earth goddesses each released a thunderbolt
and tried to crush him between the mountains.
But by his blessings their thunderbolts turned into charcoal;
their strength failed them, and the twelve goddesses,
together with the twelve tutelary ladies
and the twelve from above and from below,
gave the heart of their lives.
The Guru bound them by oath and to all of them
he entrusted a treasure.

Then he pushed on to the fort called the Bird's Nest of Oyug.
The great gaynyen Dorje Legpa Kyong
appeared amid his retinue of three hundred and sixty brothers.
Padma bound them all by an oath and left a treasure in their care.
Then, when he came to the valley of Shampo,
Shampo appeared, the white yak the size of a mountain,
from mouth and nostrils exhaling whirlwinds and snow tempests.
Using the iron hook mudrā, the Guru seized him by the muzzle,
bound him with the mudrā of the noose,
chained him with the mudrā of the shackles,
and with the bell mudrā flogged him, body and mind.
Now when the yak gave the heart of his life,
the Guru bound him by oath and entrusted him with a treasure.

To test the Guru, the spirit of the Argalis Plateau
took on the guise of a white reptile and blocked his path.
The head reached the district of the Uighurs,
while the tail coincided with the Sog River of Khams
and Gyermotang. With a staff the Guru
transfixed the serpent through the middle:
"You are the nāga king Chalk Color,

king of the gandharvas with the five hair coils.
Depart, and prepare yourself to make a circular oblation!"
The spirit fled to the ice-cold snows, but the snows melted
and, when the greenish ice had given away,
the black mountain peak could be seen.
The spirit could withstand no longer,
so he served a gaṇacakra decked out with dainties
and, changing into a child wearing a turquoise hair net
and a turban of white silk, he did obeisance and circumambulated.
He gave the heart of his life and, having been bound by oath,
he was given one hundred treasures to watch over.
As his secret name, he was called Major Vajra of Great Power.

Then, on the northern plateau,
the Guru came to the valley of Pan Yul.
Those wild northerners, the Ting Lomen Visages,
gathered together the winds of the northern regions
and loosed them on the Guru and his following.
Those with him became parched, so he attracted a cool breeze.
Then, guiding a fiery wind, like sun on butter,
he melted one of the Ting Lomen and bound him by oath.
When all of them had given the heart of their lives,
he entrusted a treasure to their care.

Then, at Lang Drom of the Heavenly Blue Juniper Trees,
Padma entered the Mandala of the Supreme Perfect Meaning
and reached Attainment. On the midnight following the seventh day,
he loosed his wrath, and when he looked,
the leaders of the army of Māra, their banners unfurled,
implored the Guru to have mercy on them.
They gave the heart of their lives, and he bound them by oath,
placing a treasure in their keeping.

Then he came to Khams, to the place called One-legged Musk Deer.
There he bound by oath all the cyclops and the other teurang.
After that he made a halt at the crag, Lion of Khams.
The being called Impure One Born from Slate,
an old man with a monkey's amice as headgear
put his head on the Guru's chest,
stretched his feet toward the Gyermotang in Khams
and raised his hands to the peaks of Kailāsa
and to Lake Manasarowar.
Ten milliard millions of nonhuman beings,
utterly unimaginable, hastened thither,
letting weapons of every kind fall like rain.
The Guru took on the fearsome aspect
of the five classes of angry deities
and all these genies were tamed,
together with their leader Born from Slate.

LODAN CHOGSED

Then the Guru reached Mount Chubo and Kharag,
where he bound by oath all the mamos and all the senmos.
After which he went to Silma in Tsang,
where he bound by oath all the mamos and all the lower gods.
At the spring of Gempa,
he obtained the submission of all the gaynyen.
At the sands of Rabka, he mastered the spirits of all eight classes.
In the speckled vale of Roha, he tamed the Ladies of the Epidemics.
In the black valley of Rong Rong, he subjugated the ogres.
In Malgro, where the nāga tribes are, he bound them by oath.
At Pugmo of the Turquoises, he bound by oath the Porgyuds.
At the Seashell Color Vermilion Rock,
he bound by oath the gandharvas.
On the snowy peaks of Kailāsa,
he subjugated the twenty-eight asterisms.
In the cavern of the Hidden Elephant, he hid yet another treasure.
At the Starsgo glacier, he subjugated the gods of the
eight great planets and the others and hid twenty-one treasures.
At the Blue Glacier, the genies prepared a circular oblation,
offering all the victuals and all the wealth of the universe.
In this glacier and at the lake of the Starsgo Glacier
he hid yet other revelatory Scriptures.
At Lobo, he bound by oath the nine Danma Sisters.
Called by the genie Pūrṇabhadra, he bound him by oath.
Called to the glacier of the Genie of the Peaks,
he bound the genie by oath.
Called by the Genie of the Heavenly Mountain,
he bound him by oath.
And to each of them Padma entrusted a treasure.

At this juncture there arrived a repeated message from the sovereign:
"The time has been fixed for the meeting
in the Todlung Drambu Park.
Triumphant and powerful king as I am,
I have dispatched many legates to you;
now only I myself have not come to you."

But for yet one more winter and one more lunar month,
the Guru resided on Mount Khalabrag.
Binding by oath the crude spirits of the mountain tops,
he entrusted to each of them a treasure.
Then he made a halt at the park of the Hermiones, at Zhul Pug.
After taming demons, planets, and the Damsri gnomes,
he gave a treasure into their keeping.
Then he dwelt for a whole spring in the Lofty Schist Mountains,
subjugating the Gongpos of the Dza ravines, and
also the Damsri at Sosha.

Padmasambhava Arrives in Tibet and Encounters the King

Then he came to Lhasa, to the Todlung pleasure park.
The king, who had taken up his abode on the bank
of the Brahmaputra,
sent Lhasang and Lupel Gyalpo as ambassadors,
with five hundred iron-clad horsemen to escort them.
Now, at the time of this encounter at Todlung Basin,
the heat was oppressive, and neither water nor tea were to be had.
But the Great One from Uḍḍiyāna, Padmasambhava,
laid his staff on the Todlung well.
"Lhasang! The water is gushing out. Hold a basin under it!" he said.
And the spot was henceforth called Divine Water of the Basin.[10]

After that, in the Double Castle in the park along the Brahmaputra's
bank, he met the ruler himself.
the king of Tibet stood forth in the midst of his court –
one might have thought it the quivering radiance
of a brood of pigeons.

The two queens appeared, surrounded by their ladies,
in dazzling attire, iridescent as tents made of samite.

For welcome there were dances with drums, dances with songs,
dances with masks, and harmonious dances.

Padma, the Great One from Uḍḍiyāna, reflected:
"I was not born from a womb; I was born by apparition;
the king was born from a womb and so by birth I am the greater.
At this instant the Law of Uḍḍiyāna lays hold on his kingdom.
This king of defiled Tibet is great through his paternal lineage.
But who are we, he and I? Plunged in darkness is his mind;
I am learned in the five realms of knowledge,
Buddha in a single lifetime, exempt from birth and death.
It is out of necessity that he invites me here.
Formerly this king bowed down before me.
Shall I or shall I not return his bow?
If yes, the majesty of the Doctrine will be slighted.
If no, since he is the king, he will be angered.
Yet, however great he be, bow down I cannot."

And King Trisong Detsen thought to himself:
"I am sovereign over all the black heads of Tibet.
The Bodhisattva Abbot has already made obeisance to me –
the Guru must prostrate himself as well."
So, loath to extend the first greeting, he stood there hesitant.

Now the Guru sang his greatness and nobility:
"The Buddhas of the Three Times passed through
the gate of the womb.
Theirs are knowledge and merit, heaped up thrice innumerable,
but I am the Buddha Padma Jungnay, Sprung from the Lotus.
Mine are the counselings that pierce the lofty concepts
of the Dharma;
I posses the precepts of the Tantric Scriptures;
I explain exhaustively, clearly distinguishing all the Vehicles.

I am Padmasambhava the Holy Doctrine.
Mine are the counselings for assured ascension in the Dharma.
Externally I am a saffron-robed bhikṣu,
and within, yogi of the supreme Secret Mantras.

I am Padmasambhava the Bhikṣu.
Mine are the counselings of the interpenetration of the theory
and practice of the Scriptures –
an intuition higher than the heavens,
more precise than the wheaten meal of retribution.

I am Padmasambhava the Lama.
Mine are the counselings that illuminate

and measure the causal data of the Doctrine.
In the book of the world and of nirvāṇa
I explain the implicit and absolute meaning.

I am Padmasambhava the Geshe.
Mine are the counselings that classify failings and virtues
in keeping with the Teachings.
I don the mantle of fivefold gnosis,
I carry the vessel of the Five Perfect Bodies of Being.

I am Padmasambhava the Abbot.
Mine are the counselings of man become Buddha;
I know the interpenetration of Inspection and Tranquility;
effortlessly I deliver the views of the Atiyoga.

I am Padmasambhava of Lofty Meditation.
Mine are the counselings on contemplating the Doctrine
outside the time of meditation.
In the circle of saṃsāra and nirvāṇa
there is no accepting or rejecting within Production or Completion.

I am Padmasambhava Master of Formulas.
Mine are the counselings for the integration
of the Production and Completion of the Dharma.
On the table of divination, as they appear in white and red,
I shall enumerate retribution's choices.

NYIMA ODZER

Padmasambhava Comes to Tibet

I am Padmasambhava the Reckoner.
Mine are the counselings of the three indivisible holy vows.
To men laid low by the sickness of the five poisons
I bring the immaculate Teachings as balm.

I am Padmasambhava the Doctor.
Mine is the nectar of the Doctrine,
the counselings that cure one of death.
And, apart from their apparition,
I raise up images identical with the gods.

I am Padmasambhava, Maker of Gods.
Mine are the counselings of the Holy Luminosities
on the Plane of Essence.
Concerning equanimity, that chart of the mind,
I write the letters that make up words to bear the meaning.

I am Padmasambhava the Scribe.
Mine are the counselings of the unwritten Teachings.
To men born on the four continents I expound archknowledge
by means of the knowledge of the Three Times.

I am Padmasambhava the Astrologer.
Mine are the counselings of the Way that leads everyone
on his own path.
Arising as enemy of the five poisons and of the five demons,
I am floodwater at the heart of the five gnoses.

I am Padmasambhava the Sorcerer.
Mine are the counselings of the Dharma
that transmutes the five poisons.
I do not bid farewell to pleasures,
I take them with me on the path.
I exult in the fivefold gnosis.

I am Padmasambhava the Bonpo.
Mine are the counselings of the Doctrine

that rewards even ill-fortune;
I bear happiness to the six orders of beings.
I have bent to my service gods and rakṣasas of the eight classes.

I am Padmasambhava the King.
Mine are the counselings of the Dharma
possessing authority in the three realms.
I embrace and shake the profound cycle of causality;
I accomplish every action, subjugating the mind itself.

I am Padmasambhava the Minister.
Mine are the counselings for entering into the Dharma,
whatever one's past deeds.
I watch over the ultimate outcome of desires;
I look at the Three Jewels without averting my gaze.

I am Padmasambhava the Queen.
Mine are the counselings of the Buddha at the hour of death.
I protect the undertakings of those who have great faith;
I make happy the subsequent life of man.

I am Padmasambhava the Lord.
Mine are the counselings of the Doctrine
that scrutinizes and pronounces upon error.
With the Bodhisattva's compassion as a blade,
I have slaughtered inimical heresy and misconception.

I am Padmasambhava the Hero.
Mine are the counselings of the Doctrine
that treads under foot the hostile cycle.
Having assigned the heritage of the three gifts,
I establish my fortunate sons in the Dharma.

I am Padmasambhava the Old Man.
Mine are the counselings of the Doctrine
that shows the Way for old men.
I escort and guide in the three moral practices;
I travel along the ways of celestial happiness.

I am Padmasambhava the Old Woman.
Mine are the counselings of the Doctrine
that gently guides old women.
I gird about me the armor of threefold patience;
I vanquish inimical misery and error.

I am Padmasambhava the Young Woman.
Mine are the counselings of the Doctrine

DORJE GROLOD

that halts the fourfold Māra.
I don the adornments of the three zeals;
I give myself as spouse to all beings.

I am Padmasambhava the Youth.
Mine are the counselings of both the relative
and absolute meaning of the Doctrine.
I storm the fortress of the threefold ecstasy;
in places of every kind I like to play.

I am Padmasambhava the Child.
Mine are the counselings of the Doctrine
that imposes silence on the denunciation of offenses.
I see by means of the threefold eye of understanding;
I nurse at the unitary knowledge of the mystic depths.

I am Padmasambhava the Little One.
Mine are the counselings of the ecstasy of the Doctrine
that rouses from sleep.
While in the three realms the transitory being dies,
I evoke that glorious Yoga, Receptacle of the Knowledge of Life.

I am Padmasambhava the Deathless.
Mine are the counselings for the diamond life of the Doctrine.
I am not dependent upon the four external elements,
nor do I set up a dwelling for the internal body of flesh and blood.

I am Padmasambhava the Unborn.
Mine are the counselings of the Great Seal of the Doctrine.
My diamond body will never wane,
for my mind, in Awakening, is perennial lucidity.

I am Padmasambhava the Ageless.
Mine are the counselings of the Dharma
that assuages the suffering
of those whose vitality yields to sickness,
whose splendid appearance has been struck down by circumstance.

Padmasambhava Comes to Tibet

I am Padmasambhava Who Knows No Sickness.
The counselings of the Great Perfection of the Dharma are mine.

And you, king of barbarian Tibet,
king of the country without virtue,
uncouth men and ogres surround you.
You rely upon famine's serfs,
and neither joy nor good humor are yours.
As for your queens, they are rakṣasī in human shape.
Beautiful purple ghouls surround them,
sandalwood, turquoise, and gold adorn them;
but they have no hearts and no minds.

You are king, your lungs swell.
Great is your power, your liver is well-satisfied.
Scepter in hand and haughty, you stand high.
But I, Sire, will not bow down before you.
And yet, in accordance with my conjoined vows,
having come to the heart of Tibet, here I stay.
Great king, witness, have I come?"

He spoke, turned his hands and, springing up from his finger
a miraculous flame seared the king's garments.
King, ministers, courtiers could not withstand him.
Bowing in unison, they prostrated themselves
as though swept by a scythe.

Padmasambhava Translates the Sutras and Tantras

Padmasambhava purified the ground to lay the foundations for the temple at Samye and then assembled all the subjugated demons and spirits. Men worked by day and non-humans by night, while the Guru sought to restore the wealth of the king's treasury. For three

nights, Padmasambhava sat in deep meditation and enjoined the nāgas to become friends with the king of Tibet. Whereupon a large serpent emerged from the lake and stirred the water, flooding the shores with waves of gold.

When the temple was finished, Padmasambhava emanated one hundred and eight simultaneous bodies and scattered blossoms throughout the one hundred and eight shrines of the temple. At once, all the sacred images came to life and strolled around the temple discussing the Dharma. The sky filled with spontaneous music, flames of fire leapt from the heads of the wrathful guardian deities who faced the four directions, and healing nectars rained from cloudless skies.

But Trisong Detsen, fearing that this Great Master of the Elements would depart, addressed the Guru saying, "Over the years, my grandfather and parents built one hundred and eight temples throughout the Himalayas. Some of these areas are so remote and difficult to reach that many have now fallen into disrepair. And the teachings, scattered far and wide, have never been gathered in one place. I will have built stūpas, written commentaries, and erected temples to no avail if, once you are here, the sacred texts of the Sūtra and Tantra cannot be brought to Tibet and completely translated."

The king, therefore, sent off a caravan of young Tibetan translators to learn Sanskrit in India from renowned teachers and to carry back the

sacred texts of the Dharma. And, though aged, Śāntarakṣita himself remained in Tibet to introduce the Sūtras and philosophical commentaries of the Hīnayāna and Mahāyāna and to train the first native-born Tibetan monks. Then, at the appropriate time, the lotsawas and paṇḍitas gathered in the central hall of the lofty Samye monastery. Guru Padmasambhava, free of the stain of birth and sprung from the lotus stalk, he who understood perfectly the meaning of all the Sūtras and Tantras, and who, having been summoned to Tibet, converted the whole land, sat cross-legged on a golden throne in the center of the temple. He was joined by the tantric scholar and master from Kashmir, Vimalamitra, who comprehended completely the texts of the Three Baskets (Tripiṭaka) and the external and internal Tantras. Then the entire assembly of eight hundred scholars began the monumental work of translating, without a single omission, the Buddhist scriptures and texts from the languages of Sanskrit, Pāli, Gilgit, and Chinese into Tibetan. Together with the learned lotsawa Vairotsana, fluent in twenty-one languages, Guru Padmasambhava translated the general and esoteric ritual Tantras and revealed the special mantra teachings of the Vajrayāna. Not even India, it has been said, could match the heights of enlightened activity that flourished at that time in Tibet.

The Guru Initiates His Close Disciples and Departs from Tibet

Many disciples matured in their understanding of the texts and practices and sought out the Precious Guru who was practicing sādhana (yogic meditation) in solitude on the upper slopes near Chimphu above Samye monastery. King Trisong Detsen, Yeshe Tsogyal, the translator Vairotsana, and others each offered the Guru a ten-ounce gold-piece shaped as a lotus flower and requested initiation into the mandala of the Unity of all Sugatas (bDe-gshegs-'dus-pa'i-dkyil-'khor). During the ritual ceremony, each of the disciples tossed a flower into the mandala to invoke the wrathful deities (Herukas) who guard the entrances to the inner circle. Identifying thoughts, feelings, and perceptions fully and actively with Guru Rinpoche, the disciples integrated their consciousness with one of his many manifestations.

Then Padmasambhava released to twenty-five close disciples the essential oral instruction, the precepts that give complete liberation from saṃsāra. For seven years they meditated before achieving the level of one-pointedness of mind through which they expressed many uncontrived and miraculous demonstrations. The king sat absorbed in samādhi, Yeshe Tsogyal resurrected a man from the dead,

SENGE DRADOG

Namkhai Nyingpo could ride on the rays of the sun, and Vairotsana attained clairvoyant insight, gaining access to all knowledge in the three moments of time.

Padmasambhava remained for a while among the Tibetan people, meditating in various caves, cemeteries, gardens, and groves and on various mountains in the Land of the Snows. Realizing that mankind was not yet ready to receive some of the highest tantric teachings, the Precious Guru imparted many scriptures that contained the essence of his teachings. At a cave near Chimphu, several miles north of Samye, these scriptures were written down by his disciples in an abbreviated and codified script that only those who were properly prepared could understand. These teachings, or Terma, were then carefully wrapped and concealed in caves and temples, at the bottom of pools, and in the cracks of rocks – and also in the Guru's Mind.[11] Knowing that the Buddhadharma could be misinterpreted and distorted by those who were not enlightened, the Uḍḍiyāna Teacher predicted that these same twenty-five disciples would later take birth as tertons, incarnate emanations of the Guru, to recover these treasures from their hiding places and to interpret the abbreviated script for the understanding of whoever required instruction.

When at last this work was completed, the Master of the Mantrayāna predicted the specific time and place of the Terma discoveries, the name of each terton, the disciple to whom the teachings would be given, and the number of people who would become enlightened throughout the Himalayas and the world as a result of their efforts. Then for twenty-one days, at Thaduk (place of the Multi-colored Dragon), he once again explained the outer, inner, and secret teachings, then commanded the king and his people to practice diligently and protect the Dharma in the future. At this time, he also advised them on a variety of subjects such as farming, law, the organization of society, and principles of enlightened governance.

A vast throng of people then escorted the Lotus-born Guru to the Gungtangla Pass on the border of Tibet, where he made his final gift to the people: the Thirteen Precepts that remove obstacles to the

continuation of the tantric lineage. Giving them his final instruction, Padmasambhava said, "May all future generations who cannot now meet me read this exposition of my spiritual practice and self-liberated existence in this world, obtain a clear view of its significance, and live according to its implied command, becoming perfect in all things." Thus exhorting the people to aspire to Buddhahood, Padmasambhava mounted a winged horse that appeared from out of the sky. Rising upwards through the mist of a radiant rainbow, the Precious Guru vanished on the rays of the sun.

From Tibet, Padmasambhava flew to the southwest land of the untamed rākṣasas and liberated them from the frustrations of saṃsaric existence. There, on the summit of the Copper-colored Mountain, he now dwells in a celestial palace. Completely compassionate, Padmasambhava, the Unoriginated Selfless One, appears in this earthly world as Bodhisattva, as Ḍākinī and wrathful deity, as mantra and as art, as Teacher, and as Buddha. The names of his manifestations and the legends surrounding them are inexhaustible. From now until the end of all suffering, his emanations labor effortlessly to ensure that all beings will finally rejoice in the ultimate realization of Buddhahood.[12]

Notes

1. Uḍḍiyāna (Oḍḍiyāna, U-dyan, or Urgyan) corresponds to an ancient territory northwest of Kashmir, but does not necessarily refer to a specific geographic location in our world system.

2. Ḍākinīs (Tib. mKha'-'gro-ma, 'sky-walker') are accomplished female beings who travel in both the sky and in the heights of pure awareness. Together with Ḍākas, their male counterparts, they exemplify the Buddhist teachings of śūnyatā.

3. Usually identified with Śrī Laṅkā.

4. Bodh Gayā, or Vajrāsana, the place where the Buddha attained enlightenment.

5. Ānanda, Buddhaguhya, (Tib. Sangs-rgyas-gsang-ba), and Śrī Siṃha are early Indian masters, and Garab Dorje (dGa'-rab rDo-rje, b. 55 CE) is the first of the Dzogchen lineage in human form. The Great Perfection (Skt. Mahāsaṃdhi, Tib. rDzogs-chen) teachings were delivered by the Buddha Vajradhara to Garab Dorje. Garab Dorje bestowed them on his pupil, Śrī Siṃha, who in turn transmitted them to Padmasambhava.

6. Lake Rewạlsar, located between the rivers Byas and Ravi in northern India, is still venerated by pilgrims as the site of Padma's miraculous transformation.

7. The realm of desire (kāmadhātu), the realm of form (rūpadhātu), and the formless realm (arūpadhātu).

8. Samye is situated about thirty miles southeast of Lhasa at an altitude of 11,500 feet.

9. The following three cantos (LIX-LXI) appear in the Padma Tanyig (Padma-thang-yig) attributed to Yeshe Tsogyal. This text is a celebrated Tibetan account of Padmasambhava's life (rnam-thar), a treasure teaching (gter-ma) recovered in the mid-fourteenth century. G.-C. Toussaint translated the Tibetan into French (Le Dict de Padma, Paris: 1933) and Kenneth Douglas translated the French into English (*The Life and Liberation of Padmasambhava,* edited by Tarthang Tulku. Berkeley: Dharma Publishing, 1978.)

10. Visitors to this place report that water still flows out of solid rock in a stream about one inch in diameter from a point approximately eight feet above the ground.

11. Through the discovery of these revitalizing scriptures (gter-ma), the Nyingmapa constantly regenerate their tradition. "In Tibet the principle of continuing revelation takes three forms: the rediscovery of texts and holy objects (sa-gter) buried by Padmasambhava and his colleagues for revelation at a future time, the spontaneous appearance of teachings which were concealed in the Guru's Mind for propagation by future emanations (dgongs-gter), and instructions passed on by manifestations of gurus and tutelaries in visions (dag-snang)." (E. Gene Smith, preface to *The Autobiographical Reminiscences of Ngag-dbang-dpal-bzang.* Gangtok, 1969) Terma hidden in the Guru's Mind are accessible only during profound meditation, when the clouds of mental obscurity have been dissolved and the structure of being is clearly visible. Terma found in natural phenomena may be discovered by such events as the sudden spontaneous bursting open of a rock that discloses a cipher key. See *The Legend of the Great Stupa,* cited below.

12. Longer accounts of Padmasambhava's life and teachings may be found in the following:

Dudjom Jig-dral Ye-shes rDo-rje, gSang-sngags-snga-'gyur-rnying-ma-pa'i bstan-pa'i rnam-gzhag-mdo-tsam-brjod-pa-legs-bshad snang-ba'i dga'-ston *[rNying-ma'i chos-'byung, The History of the Nying-ma- pa].* Kalimpong, 1967. Now available in English: *The*

Nyingma School of Tibetan Buddhism: Its Fundamentals and History, translated and edited by Gyurme Dorje with the collaboration of Matthew Kapstein. Boston: Wisdom Publications, 1991. 2 volumes.

Evans-Wentz, W. Y. (ed). *The Tibetan Book of the Great Liberation*. London, New York, Toronto: Oxford University Press, 1954.

Tarthang Tulku (ed.). *The Legend of the Great Stupa*, translated by Keith Dowman. Berkeley: Dharma Publishing, 1973. Second edition, revised, 2004.

Tarthang Tulku (ed.). *The Life and Liberation of Padmasambhava*, translated by Kenneth Douglas. Berkeley: Dharma Publishing, 1978.

Toussaint, G.-C. (trans.). *Le Dict de Padma (Padma Thang Yig, MS. de Lithang)*. Paris, 1933.

TSOKYI DORJE

URGYAN DORJE CHANG

ŚĀKYA SENGE

PADMASAMBHAVA

LODAN CHOGSED

PADMA GYALPO

NYIMA ODZER

DORJE DROLOD

SENGE DRADOG

PADMASAMBHAVA

Twenty-five Disciples of Padmasambhava

PADMASAMBHAVA AND TWENTY-FIVE DISCIPLES

Just as the teachings of Lord Buddha were passed on with great care from master to disciple, the tantric teachings were successfully transmitted to Tibet in the eighth century by Padmasambhava. During the subsequent suppression of Buddhism in Tibet (described on p. 117), the Great Guru's twenty-five principal disciples preserved the sacred texts and oral instructions through their spiritual and clan lineages. Thus they became the first generation of Nyingma practitioners, progenitors of a lineage that has continued unbroken for twelve centuries down to the present time.

Upon Padmasambhava's arrival in Tibet, word was secretly spread among the King's ministry that a superior Master of the Vajrayāna had come to instruct others in the Way of the Diamond Path. Soon the Lotus-born Guru attracted followers who showed their sincerity by engaging in the practice of his teachings. Eventually there appeared those who demonstrated superior capacities, and to them the Guru gave private instructions and taught advanced forms of meditation and sādhana. Realizing the richness and profundity of the Dharma teachings, many of these disciples participated in the work of translating the Sūtras and Tantras.

At a significant moment in their relationship, the disciples approached the Guru and offered him ritual gifts representing the actions of body, speech, and mind. As Padmasambhava himself relates in *The Legend of the Great Stupa*:

"While I was practicing sādhana in solitude on the upper slopes near Chimphu, above the monastery of Samye Ling, King Trisong Detsen... and others of the twenty-five disciples came to me and presented offerings of gold and other precious gifts, entreating me to unfold the mandala of the Unity of All Buddhas. After I had disclosed the mandala, I gave them initiation."

Thereafter, each of the twenty-five disciples perfected a particular aspect of Padmasambhava's teaching that stimulated specific meditative abilities. Each disciple, then, has come to be known by a specific gesture, as illustrated by the thanka details reproduced in this chapter. The biographies that accompany them are also intended to provide convenient points of entry into these portrayals, for each pictorial metaphor draws our attention to the integral wholeness of the mind and its external manifestations – qualities that are neither easily expressed nor experienced.

The lives of the twenty-five disciples provide us with rich examples of properly motivated activity – an aspiration for enlightenment unhampered by pretenses. To enter the mandala of the dynamic presence of the Guru, each of the disciples made a ritual offering of his body, speech and mind, indicated by the casting of a flower into the center of the mandala. Symbolizing a sacrifice of the whole of one's being, such an offering represents a priceless gift to the Guru.

To enter a mandala, either physically or as a totally internalized visualization, is a very significant act. One's entire being – one's thoughts, feelings, and perceptions – are fully and actively engaged. Rather than make the pursuit of enlightenment into some idealized future project, the meditator chooses to give of himself completely here and now. Nothing is held back. Without this basic willingness to surrender all our notions of who we think we are and what we think is possible for us, genuine freedom is impossible.

For this reason, many Buddhist teachings focus attention on the deceptive nature of desire. Desire can entrap us in self-centered craving, or it can lead us to recognize our bodily limitations and thus yearn to exchange this world for some illusion concerning the 'infinite' and 'transworldly'. Entry into the mandala, however, demands the death of all desire, and this death permits the birth of an appreciative commitment to the intensity of life just as it unfolds.

'Entering', then, is not possible without 'offering'. Entry into any of the stages of Buddhist development involves the taking of vows by those who are guided by the motivation to attain enlightenment in this lifetime. This vow is not something we must carry out with a blind sense of duty. It is the natural outflow of a firm commitment to be true to who we are, without succumbing to any selective biases concerning our 'development'. If we must have a 'view' at all, only an enlightened one will do.

This aspiration for enlightenment, which evokes the transfiguration of all generally frustrating constituents of saṃsāra, is further illumined by a living exemplar, the Guru-as-Reality, who, as the embodiment of enlightened consciousness, is uncompromisingly awake and compassionately active. At the moment of initiation, each of the disciples accepted as his or her exemplar one of eight guardian Herukas who elucidate various aspects of the mind of Guru Rinpoche. While our timid personalities are normally confined to the realms of fiction, the wrathful deities, or Herukas, are not similarly constrained to some fictional 'beyond'. They stride over all boundaries and thrive on the nourishment of all circumstances. Their power derives from their fierce practicality and their immunity to the seductiveness of inauthentic uses of body, speech, and mind. Their bodily action – the spontaneously kept commitment to reality – suggests the nature of the very advanced sādhana practiced by the twenty-five disciples. Similarly, by means of this internal transformation, their speech expresses the essential quality of mantra, which communicates the intrinsic value of life present in every situation. Through mantra, the mind becomes relaxed, concentrated and fully appreciative, able to envision all manifestations of body, speech, and mind as essentially perfect.

Calling upon a 'tutelary deity' or inner guide awakens within us our own deep connections with this enlightened consciousness. For example, propitiation of Hayagrīva (the wrathful aspect of Amitābha, Lord of Boundless Light) empowers the initiate to subdue the impure mental forces of passion-lust. Propitiation of Vajrakīla (the wrathful manifestation of the 'fearless' Amoghasiddhi) severs the roots of karmically inherited dispositions that stem from envy-jealousy, insecurity, fear, and self-condemnation, To call upon one's Heruka is, therefore, to bring the enlightenment of the Guru – who spans all circumstances – into a meaningful relation with the immediate events of one's own life. This process of integration produces a new vision and fresh perspective whereby the individual apprehends the world surrounding him and all that it contains as a total presence – an harmoniously interrelated field seen as the embodiment of absolute being.

Padmasambhava's followers accomplished this integration to such a degree that their actions appeared to be magical to those unwilling to believe that such spontaneous and inspired activity might constitute an appropriate norm for everyone. Their display of paranormal powers or abilities, such as drawing water from rocks, indicates that beyond a rational system of conceptual interpretations there exists a level of reality where an unprejudiced awareness operates freely within the open, undefined parameters of immediately lived experience. Once this underlying awareness was discovered and developed, the disciples recognized the material world as neither fixed nor solid. By contemplating the transitoriness of all phenomenal existence, they learned to penetrate material substances – as shown by such feats as passing through rocks – as easily as they could penetrate the most subtle regions of mind itself. Neither magicians nor metaphorical 'deities', the disciples manifested the effects of their direct realization through their subsequent activity in the world. The images depicted here only point in a symbolic way to this realization. They represent mere drops in the ocean of possibility.

I have compiled the following short biographies from the Tibetan accounts in Dudjom Rinpoche's Chos-byung (see p. 44), Kongtrul Lodro Thaye's Encyclopedia, and from my own memory based on the teachings of my guru, Jamyang Khyentse Lodro. These twenty-five disciples – and their disciples – are also responsible for a great number of the early translations of the Sūtras and śāstras that appear in the Tibetan Canon, as well as many original and compiled works appearing in the collection of Nyingma Tantras known as the Nyingma Gyudbum. Even today many scholars are not aware of the sizeable contributions made by Vairotsana, Kawa Paltseg, Yeshe De, Chokro Lui Gyaltsen, Ma Rinchen Chok, and other early Nyingma translators, so I hope it will be useful and informative to introduce their names to the West.

Throughout the centuries, many great precious masters (rin-po-che) from all the schools of Tibetan Buddhism have benefited from the preservation and oral transmission of Nyingma meditation practices and initiations. May the memory and subtle power of this ancient and direct lineage now be planted and shared with all people, fulfilling the prophecy of Padmasambhava that the teachings of the Vajrayāna would one day bloom throughout the world.

Trisong Detsen

As Tibet's most powerful king, Trisong Detsen (c. 755–97 C.E.) extended his territories well beyond the Tibetan frontiers and maintained political influence over one-third of the known world. But nothing could satisfy him more than fulfilling his desire to unify the teachings of the Buddha in the Land of the Snow-capped Peaks. So he invited the Bodhisattva Abbot Śāntarakṣita to instruct the Tibetans in the meaning of the Sūtras, the practice of the sixteen moral precepts, and the basic mental trainings of Mahāyāna Buddhism. Convinced of the great value of the Buddhist teachings, Trisong Detsen then invited the Uḍḍiyāna Master, the renowned Guru Padmasambhava, who brought with him the inner teachings of the Tantras and the oral instructions of the Mantrayāna. Padmasambhava initiated the king together with his other advanced disciples into the mandala of the Unity of all Buddhas, wherein the king offered a golden flower to Chemchok Heruka in the center of the mandala.[1] Through his practice of sādhana, the king integrated his behavior and awareness with that of Hayagrīva and awakened into samādhi.[2]

King Trisong Detsen carefully studied the texts that Śāntarakṣita had brought to Tibet. Determined to translate the Indian texts and teachings into Tibetan, he sent more than a hundred Tibetans to learn Sanskrit in India. Their task completed, they returned to Tibet bearing numerous sacred texts and accompanied by scores of Indian paṇḍitas. Then, together with Vimalamitra,[3] Vairotsana, and other outstanding masters, they translated Sūtras, Tantras, and commentaries in the Great Hall at Samye monastery.

The king, however, whose clan of De belonged to the ancient Bon tradition, found it increasingly difficult to justify the presence of the Indian teachers and scholars to his royal ministers, high ranking courtiers who performed specialized religious, social, and political functions. These ministers, feeling their position threatened by the authority and prestige given to the king's Buddhist guests, accused the king of being tricked by the Indian magicians into depleting the royal treasury in order to build Samye monastery. "Of what value," they asked, "are the Buddhists? They waste our resources and make food-offerings to their wrathful deities that are never eaten." Rather than relinquish their power, the king's ministers persistently counseled him against the Buddhists, saying, "You are a Bonpo and Bon is a venerable tradition. There is no reason for you to invite these Indian teachers and threaten the social order in Tibet." Even the foreign relatives of Trisong Detsen's queens opposed the Indian paṇḍitas and demanded their departure. Not knowing how to resolve this conflict, the king was advised to sponsor a debate to determine which group was more worthy to direct the religious activity of Tibet. The Bonpos, thinking that they possessed the most eloquent and intellectual speakers and convinced that their psychic capacities were significantly advanced, publicized the debate widely.

When the debate was scheduled to take place, the disciples of Padmasambhava, who had been meditating in caves and in the surrounding mountains, gathered together near Lhasa. A tent made of cotton was erected in a place called Dragmar Rinzang. Here Trisong Detsen appointed judges, both Bonpo and Buddhist, from among the large assembly, and gave them their charge: "Everyone observe what is true and what is false, and who has the greater magical powers. Once and for all, the Bonpos and Buddhists must contest their skills." Thus the contest began.

The Buddhist disciples were prepared. Their intense practice had nurtured and stabilized in them a deep understanding that all appearance arises and remains within an open horizon of possibilities. With limitless freedom, they displayed myriad signs of their spiritual development.

The teacher Padmasambhava hung his cloak over the sun's rays
when the sun rose in the morning.
The Bodhisattva Śāntarakṣita threw a thunderbolt
into space that stayed there for a day.
Namkhai Nyingpo left his rosary hanging in mid-air.
Palgyi Senge drew rainbow figures in space.
Gyalway Lodro caught wild animals and milked them.
Sogpo Lhapal made tigers, leopards, and brown bears tame as dogs.
Ma Rinchen Chok sat cross-legged in space.
Kawa Paltseg cut off his head and put it back again.
Vairotsana's swift-footedness equaled that of a bird.
Gyalwa Changchub stood a vase in mid-air.
Konchog Jungnay sat in a bonfire without being burned.

After this amazing display of skill, the king summoned all of his ministers and said, "Since this holy Buddhadharma is good for both here and hereafter, I urge you to follow it." He thereby ruled for the Buddhists to remain. The Bonpos, in their books, claim that they also performed marvelous displays, but, as the king wanted to practice Buddhism, they had no choice but to concede. Thus many Bonpos became Buddhists. From that time on, the twenty-five disciples of Padmasambhava were recognized as true masters of the Mantrayāna.

Trisong Detsen, regarded as an incarnation of Mañjusrī, received Padmasambhava's complete teachings and became Guru Rinpoche's direct successor, passing on the Dzogchen instructions called Slob-dpon-chen-po Pad-ma'i bka'-sgrol. He wrote commentaries on the Sūtras, practiced the tantric teachings, and meditated in the awareness of perpetual samādhi. In subsequent years, scholars and translators arriving from India brought many precious relics and jewels. With these, Trisong Detsen initiated the work of restoring the 108 temples that had been constructed throughout Tibet in the time of Songtsen Gampo. Thus, under the direction of Trisong Detsen, the Doctrine spread across the country like daylight at dawn.

Yeshe Tsogyal

Originally one of Trisong Detsen's young queens, Yeshe Tsogyal became one of Padmasambhava's closest disciples. In the initiation mandala, her flower-offering fell upon Dorje Phurbu (Vajrakīla) who revealed to her the intrinsic awareness (ye-shes) radiant with all positive qualities. From Padmasambhava she received the name Tsogyal, 'Ruler of the Lake', and she mastered the Guru's complete teachings. Out of compassion for a mother grieving for her dead son, she restored the young man to life. For the rest of her long life, she was renowned for her great compassion and liberated many sentient beings from the misery of the lower realms.

Yeshe Tsogyal often conversed with Guru Rinpoche, asking many questions and writing down his words. In this way, she requested the essence of the tantric teachings. Then, with an unfailing memory, she transcribed his teachings and reduced their meaning to symbolic

form in a codified script known only to the inner circle of initiates. She prepared these 'treasure texts', or Terma, on yellow parchment; some were abbreviated to a single page while others were much more extensively detailed and extended over many folios. Thousands of treasure texts, carefully wrapped to protect them from the ravages of weather and natural deterioration, were concealed in specific locations designated by Padmasambhava.

After Padmasambhava's departure from Tibet, Yeshe Tsogyal collaborated with Sangye Yeshe to transcribe many more volumes of Guru Rinpoche's instructions, including Padma's biography, the Padma Tanyig. Wherever she went, in all parts of Tibet and Nepal, she taught the Vajra Guru Mantra and encouraged all she met to cultivate the intention to attain Enlightenment. Revered as an incarnation of Sarasvatī, goddess of learning, aesthetic beauty, and eloquence, she lived on this earth for over two hundred years, then disappeared in a radiance of rainbow light to join Padmasambhava on the Copper-colored Mountain. She left no mortal remains.

Because she is identical with Padmasambhava, all initiations, Terma masters, and siddhis come through Yeshe Tsogyal. Through her continuous compassionate activity, she awakens awareness in the hearts of those who recite the Vajra Guru Mantra and practice the teachings of Guru Rinpoche.

Vairotsana

Vairotsana Vairotsana was one of Padmasambhava's most gifted disciples. He was born into the Pagor clan in Zangkor near Lhasa and practiced meditation in caves, unattached to the extremes of misery or happiness. It is said that at the age of eight he left the imprint of his foot imbedded in a rock at Nemo as a sign of his spiritual attainments. One of the original seven monks trained by Śāntarakṣita, Vairotsana was sent to India by Trisong Detsen. Thereafter, he traveled widely in India, China, Khotan, and elsewhere, receiving teachers from more than twenty-five masters. From Śrī Siṃha, he received the secret doctrines of the Atiyoga. As the master wrote them down in goat's milk on a white cloth, he told Vairotsana, "If you hold the cloth over smoke, the letters will become quite visible, but you must carefully guard the secret teachings." When Vairotsana returned to Tibet, he became one of the most respected translators of his time, wording the teachings of the Buddha with precision and insight. Afterwards, guided by Padmasambhava, he edited the eight Nyingma Heruka sādhanas, including the cycles of Vajrakīla and Hayagrīva.

When Guru Rinpoche initiated him into the Maṇḍala of the Self-same Nature of All Buddhas, Vairotsana cast his golden flower on Dragnag Heruka (Mod-pa Drag-sngags). Thereafter, he practiced meditation ceaselessly and received many private teachings and advanced practices. Contemplating that the nature of phenomenal existence has no origination and no characteristic marks, Vairotsana became inseparable from Guru Rinpoche, who said to him, "As I am, so are you."

Cherishing and utilizing the spontaneous appearances of the mind's projections, Vairotsana mastered the three classes of Mahāsaṃdhi precepts (Man-ngag rDzogs-pa-chen-po) as handed down by the Ācāryas Śāntiṃgarbha, Hūṃkāra and Vimalamitra: (i) the mental class (sems-sde), unveiling the apparitional nature of phenomenality; (ii) the class of relativity (klong-sde), or 'vastness teachings', removing all mental judgments through meditation on śūnyatā; and (iii) the precept class (man-ngag-gi-sde), or 'direct methods' of the Nyingtig, which provides the 'fulfillment instructions' for the practice of Mantrayāna.

After meditating for many years in Kham, Vairotsana carried the tantric teachings to China. His unclouded devotion and faith opened his inner eye and enabled him to see both the formed and formless as the manifestation of unoriginated awareness. Among his reincarnations was the renowned master Kongtrul Lodro Thaye.

Sangye Yeshe

Born in the fertile region of Nub in western Tibet, and initiated by Padmasambhava into the Mandala of the Wrathful Herukas, Sangye Yeshe cast his golden flower upon Yamāntaka, who reveals the impermanence underlying all phenomenal existence. While he was practicing the Mantrayāna teachings in the secluded caves above Samye monastery, he visualized Yamāntaka and Mañjuśrī. Suddenly, all the deities of the Yamāntaka Mandala spontaneously appeared before him. Through his practice of the Vajrakīla sādhana, he pierced the restrictive nature of common appearance and became able to shatter rocks with a touch of his mystic daggar (phur-bu). Absorbing into his body the rays of the sun and moon, he discovered within himself the light of transcending awareness. From these attainments he became widely known as a great siddha.

During the suppression of Buddhism under Langdarma, Sangye Yeshe traveled across the Himalayas seven times to visit learned teachers in Nepal and India. There he studied and translated Mahāyāna Sūtras and Nyingma Tantras and imparted the oral teachings of Guru Rinpoche. His practice reached full maturity when he mastered the three unsurpassable yogas, Mahā, Anu, and Ati. So successful and fearless was he that one day the King Langdarma, hearing of the great 'magic man', invited Sangye Yeshe to his court. "What sort of power do you have?" he asked. "Show me your power." Sangye Yeshe accepted the challenge. Pointing his finger toward the sky, he chanted a mantra. Suddenly a huge scorpion, larger than a yak, stood balanced on his fingertips. Langdarma looked stunned, but Sangye Yeshe was not yet finished. "Look," he said, and from the scorpion (a swallower of evil) came a thunderbolt that pulverized the nearby rocks into sand. The demonstration was sufficient to terrify Langdarma, who pledged not to disturb the Ngakpa (sngags-pa), the long-haired lay followers of the Mantrayāna.

Sangye Yeshe is an important link in the transmission of the Nyingma lineage. Together with Yeshe Tsogyal, he compiled many of Guru Rinpoche's teachings and preserved innumerable texts in his private library during Langdarma's short but violent reign. Following his death at the age of 113 years, his disciples continued to transmit the tantric teachings, especially the practice of the Vajrakīla sādhana.

Gyalwa Choyang

Born into the Namlam clan near Palyul, in eastern Tibet, Gyalwa Choyang was one of the Bodhisattvas trained by Śāntarakṣita. Respected for his purity as a monk, he offered the flower of his body, speech, mind, and action into the Mandala of the Herukas, becoming identical with the Horse-headed One, Hayagrīva so completely that the neighing of a horse was often heard emanating from the crown of his head. He dissolved all karmic inclinations by practicing the meditation that is beyond speech, the object of no-thought, the 'horse of non-action,' which neither comes nor goes. Through perfect understanding of the inseparability of form and formlessness, he radiated the light of original awareness, represented by Amitābha, and was able to transmute his body into a raging fire. During his life, Gyalwa Choyang performed many services for King Trisong Detsen and learned to blend every action into the path of immediate, lived freedom.

Namkhai Nyingpo

Born into the clan of Nub, Namkhai Nyingpo was among the most important of the early Nyingma translators and practitioners of the Mantrayāna teachings. He traveled to India several times, once to master the art of translation and a second time to receive initiation from the great siddha Hūmkāra. Offering a flower in the shape of a golden heart, Namkhai Nyingpo entered the Initiation Mandala of Yandak Heruka, who unites the non-discursive knowledge and spontaneous action of the Buddha. As a result of his practice, he became able to ride on the rays of the sun in the sky of intrinsic awareness.

One day in early spring, his nephew asked him for some seeds to plant because the farmers' supplies were depleted. Namkhai Nyingpo replied, "If the farmers have no seed, where can I, a yogi, find some?" But taking some small rocks, he instructed his nephew to pulverize

them and plant the granules. Soon many varieties of flowers, plants, and vegetables could be seen sprouting from the ground.

Namkhai Nyingpo was accustomed to flying wherever he traveled. One day this great disciple's prayer beads fell from the sky into a certain valley. When his fingers, in picking up the beads, touched the earth, five fragrant flowers appeared. From the center of the flowers emerged five Ḍākinīs who in turn erected five stūpas, which exist to this day.

It was not uncommon for his disciples to bring him food offerings and ask for his blessing. On one occasion, he gave them tiny stones in return that turned into precious turquoise, empowering each of them with the sky-like realization.

Exiled at the instigation of the Bonpo nobles, this great master went into retreat at Lodrak Karchu. Attaining realization through practice of the Yandak Heruka sādhana, he left this world embraced in the radiance of rainbow light.

Yeshe Zhonnu

Born into the Nyak clan in Yarlung, Yeshe Zhonnu was generally known as Nyak Jñānakumāra, Prince of Knowledge. At his birth, two black moles in the shape of a double dorje (viśvavajra) appeared on his throat, signifying his complete detachment from the self-seeking and pride of worldly existence. Ordained by Śāntarakṣita, Yeshe Zhonnu worked with Indian paṇḍitas at Samye to translate many Sūtras and śāstras preserved in the Kanjur and Tanjur. As a practitioner of Mantrayāna, he became the disciple of both Vimalamitra and Padmasambhava and received teachings from Vairotsana and Ugra Nyingpo. Upon his initiation into the Nyingma Heruka sādhanas by Padmasambhava, he entered the center of the mandala, propitiating Chemchog Heruka and drinking the pure water of spiritual instruction. From Vimalamitra he received transmission of the Vajrakīla sādhana. His study of the Phurbu

tradition heightened his unwavering awareness and strengthened his extraordinary powers to the point where healing nectars flowed from rocks at his touch. Once when he was staying in a cave at Yarlung with Gyalwa Choyang, Yeshe Zhonnu took the form of a crow to see if Gyalwa Choyang would recognize him. Another time he projected himself as a baby camel and playfully pranced around the meditation cave. But both times Gyalwa Choyang immediately realized who it was and greeted his friend.

Holder of the major streams of the Mahā–, Anu–, and Atiyoga teachings, Yeshe Zhonnu was a key link in the transmission of the Nyingma lineages, which flowed from him through an unbroken succession of outstanding masters.

Palgyi Yeshe

Born into the clan of Drok ('Brog) near Shantag, Palgyi Yeshe studied and translated the Nyingma Tantras assiduously, particularly the Mamo Bodtong. In the unfolding of the initiation mandala, his flower fell on Lhamed Heruka. When the full mandala spontaneously appeared before him, all restless tendencies of body, speech, and mind were consumed in the great fire of intrinsic awareness. With a fiery glance he destroyed self-created obstacles and released both human and non-human spirits from the lower realms of suffering and depression, teaching them watchfulness and attention to immanent death. He practiced meditation on the peaks of snow-encrusted mountains of the southern Yarlung Valley and trained many accomplished disciples and lamas. In later times he reincarnated as the terton Dechen Lingpa.

Palgyi Senge

Born into the clan of Lang (rLangs), Palgyi Senge was the son of Changchub Dekhol, who, at the age of eight, traveled throughout the mountains and subdued many wild demons in Uḍḍiyāna at the invitation of Gesar, king of Ling. One of the 108 lotsāwas sent to India by Trisong Detsen, Palgyi Senge became the heart-son of Guru Rinpoche. Through his earnest practice of the Jigten Chodto (Praise of the World) sādhana, he understood the interrelation of causes and conditions and surrendered completely the neurotic craving that accumulates frustrating karma. On one occasion he visited the lower realms and liberated many human and non-human beings from the bewilderments of clouded judgment. A layman, Palgyi Senge fathered three sons from two wives and passed on the tantric teachings through his clan lineage. For a long time he practiced meditation in the Himalayas near Bhutan, offering to all the nectar of spiritual instruction.

Dorje Dudjom

Born into the clan of Tsarung, Dorje Dudjom was serving as one of Trisong Detsen's ministers when Śāntarakṣita and Padmasambhava arrived in Tibet. One day, as he was meditating in a completely dark cave, he saw in a vision that the construction of the temple at Samye was nearing completion. He somehow managed to emerge from the sealed cave through a small chink in the rock, leaving behind a large passageway that can still be seen today. He became a disciple of Padmasambhava. During his initiation into the Unity Mandala, his flower fell on Jigten Chodto ('Jig-rten mChod-stod) Heruka. While practicing the Vajrakīla sādhana in the mountains near Samye, he cut off thoughts at the root and demonstrated his attainment by sticking his phurbu in a rock. By allowing self-existing mind to assume its natural state, he could walk in space as free as the wind, traveling to other continents with the speed of a moment's thought.

In later life, he returned to Tsarung, where he translated many tantric

texts and communicated the Mantrayāna teachings to the lineage of his clan at the red rock called the Bird's Nesting Place. Through his control of breath and mental events, he passed from this life, having realized the relative, ungraspable nature of all things. He later reincarnated as Rigzin Goddem, one of the three great Terma kings, and in recent times as Jamyang Khyentse Wangpo.[4]

Yeshe Yang

Yeshe Yang was one of eight manuscript editors who transcribed Guru Rinpoche's private inner teachings. While deep in meditation, he understood the arising and vanishing of thoughts in the sky-like expanse of mind, and his awareness extended beyond space and time to the realm of no-thought. In this lucidity of mind-itself, he traveled throughout space to the realm of the Ḍākinīs and received the eloquent ciphers appropriate to the recording of the Termas. Following Padmasambhava's directions, he concealed many of these oral teachings – direct manifestations of the Guru's Mind – in various secret places such as rocks, deep pools, caves, and the sky. Sometimes called Bandhe, or teacher, he was known and respected for his clear and exact manner of expression. He released himself from all worldly entanglements and resided for a time in the forested mountainsides with Sogpo Lhapal. One day, he flew up into the sky and disappeared.

Sogpo Lhapal

A layman metalsmith, Sogpo Lhapal was physically very powerful, working cross-legged in the traditional fashion with a crude bellows and a charcoal fire. He was befriended by Yeshe Zhonnu, who delivered to him the tantric texts and their oral commentaries. Through practice of the inner sādhana of Vajrakīla, he purified the analytical powers of his mind. Three times, while sitting in front of his meditation cave, he subdued the prideful enemies of his own thought creations. With fierce mastery of ignorance and illusion, he fearlessly restrained even wild tigers. He lived outdoors in the forests along running mountain streams until he passed away.

Yeshe De

Born into the clan of Nanam, Yeshe De was one of the four greatest early Nyingma translators.[5] As a young monk, his scholarship earned him the title of Bandhe. He was ever sensitive to the subtle nuances and precise shades of meaning in the hundreds of texts that he translated, and he played a key role in the transmission of Abhidharma and Prajñāpāramitā. Like Longchenpa, Yeshe De comprehensively studied the Nyingma Tantras and sādhanas. A master of the Vajrakīla Tantra, he realized the illusory character of phenomenal appearances and cut the cord of mind-made karmic conditioning, leaving him free to soar in the sky like a bird. Masters of the Nanam Phurbu lineage he transmitted continue the Vajrakīla sādhana practice to this day.

Karchen Palgyi Wangchuk

As a son emulates his father, Palgyi Wangchuk, brother of Yeshe Tsogyal, discovered in his practice the essential meaning of the Great Guru's instruction and became known as the 'heart son' of Guru Rinpoche. Uniting mantra and mudrā, he is shown holding aloft the phurbu and subduing the illusory objects of phenomena with the blade of discriminating awareness. Simply by raising his phurbu, he could direct feverish heat waves toward his enemies, pacifying them at once and eliminating every obstruction to complete spiritual understanding. An invulnerable lay master, Palgyi Wangchuk traveled throughout Tibet in company with his sister and Padmasambhava. Wherever he went, he communicated the oral teachings (bKa'-ma) of the early Nyingmapa.

Danma Tsemang

Born in Danma in the eastern province of Kham, Tsemang fashioned the elegant handwritten calligraphy of Tibetan script. A precise Sanskrit scholar, he was especially skilled in deciphering notes appended to the Sanskrit texts, perceiving their intended meanings through the depth of his understanding. Tsemang was able to recite with perfect recollection the Sūtras and Tantras for days at a time and thus attained the clarity of the non-dual mind unobscured by the distinctions of time and space. Having studied the tantric texts, he went into retreat in the forests and mountains, where he practiced sādhanas in the sacred caves.

Numerous manuscripts written by his hand and discovered by Terma masters are still preserved in Tibet.

Kawa Paltseg

At an early age, the lotsawa Kawa Paltseg was recognized by Padmasambhava as the reincarnation of an Indian mahāpaṇḍita, purposely born in Tibet in order to translate the texts necessary for the successful transmission of Buddhism. Born in Pembo north of Lhasa, he was one of the first seven Tibetan monks ordained and trained in the Vinaya by Śāntarakṣita. At Samye, he became one of the three most influential of the early translators. Under Padmasambhava's guidance, Kawa Paltseg studied the tantric teachings and attained a state of peace, composure, and harmony whereby his range of vision was not only widened but perfectly cleared. With awareness unclouded by habitual thought patterns, able to see past and future simultaneously, he received through the power of clairvoyance pure all-encompassing knowledge.

In addition to his numerous translations, Kawa Paltseg wrote

significant commentaries on the tantric texts. His style of calligraphy was widely imitated in all of Tibet, and through his lineage many Nyingma tertons discovered hidden treasures.

Shudbu Palgyi Senge

Born into Trisong Detsen's clan and a student of the Bon tradition, Shudbu Palgyi Senge was sent by the king to invite Padmasambhava to Tibet. After investigating the many branches of learning available in Sanskrit texts, he returned to Tibet to become one of eight renowned scholars. Following Padmasambhava's instruction, he practiced the Shinje, Mamo and Phurbu Tantras (Father, Mother and Non-dual Tantras), thereby transcending subjectively experienced negative energies and karmic forces.

Through his practice, Palgyi Senge acquired many siddhis. One day, wishing to cross a wide, swift-running river, he touched the water with his phurbu. Immediately, the waters of the river parted and exposed a passageway, allowing him to walk on the river bedto the opposite shore. Another time, placing his phurbu on a rock,

he walked directly through the stone to the other side. Once, at Chimphu near Samye, when he displayed the Vajrakīla mudrā, the river began to flow upwards.

In jest, he often referred to his birth among the Bonpos and would say, "I am descended from the heaven-clan, out of the sky!" He took an active part in the decoration of Samye temple and built an enormous white stūpa on its eastern side. As people gathered around, he sank a long wooden pipe into the soil. Through this pipe a rich buttery oil oozed up from the earth, and he distributed it to everyone for their tea.

Palgyi Senge is counted as one of the eight greatest Tibetan scholars as well as an accomplished Mantrayāna practitioner. Over the years, he practiced meditation in various caves, and his clan lineage generated many successful masters and monks. Biographies of Palgyi Senge, as well as many of the texts he translated, are still available today.

Gyalway Lodro

Originally one of Trisong Detsen's administrators, Gyalway Lodro traveled to India and became a monk. Learning Sanskrit, he studied with Hūṃkāra, one of the eighty-four mahāsiddhas. In Tibet, he received from Padmasambhava the oral teachings that grant freedom from all saṃsaric tendencies and bestow the inner elixir of youth.

Through meditation on the non-dual nature of mind that encompasses all realms and embraces all inhabitants, Gyalway Lodro rescued his mother and many others from the death-realms of the Yamarājas and turned their corpses into solid gold. These treasures he stored in caves and statues where various tertons later discovered them. Through his propitiation of Yangdag Heruka, he acquired the faculty of longevity. He lived in the forests and mountains, practicing the teachings and transmitting them to others for over three hundred years.

Khye'u Chung Lotsawa

Recognized as an incarnation of an Indian mahāpaṇḍita, Khye'u Chung Lotsawa was born into the clan of Brog and learned Sanskrit without effort at an early age. Padmasambhava instructed him in many esoteric tantric teachings, and through his practice he became widely known as an all-encompassing master of the Mantrayāna. He immediately comprehended that which is beyond the domain of discursive thought, and freed himself from all limitations through unclouded devotion and faith. By means of mudrā (ritual gestures) he was able to attract and catch flying birds and teach them the transient nature of all phenomena.

A layman (sngags-pa), he lived in the warm fertile valleys of eastern Tibet and later reincarnated as Terchen Duddul Dorje Lingpa, the Terma master of Katog monastery.

Tenpa Namkha

While attending the debates between the Bonpos and Padmasambhava's disciples, Tenpa Namkha demonstrated that a person who had attained realization had no need to distinguish between the Bonpos and Buddhists. Rising up in the sky, he struck the moon and sun together like a pair of cymbals. "There is no need," he said, "to introduce distinctions into the shining knowledge of the mutual sphere of sentient beings." Revered by the Bonpos as a manifestation of their founder, Tenpa Namkha cut off a lock of his hair with a gold razor and was initiated into the circle of the Mantrayāna by Padmasambhava. Afterwards, he meditated in the woods and mountains and developed the completely awakened state, free from the agitation of phenomenal forms. Through gestures and mudrās alone, he tamed the wild yak of the northern plains and taught many other beings roaming in the realms of restless existence. He is said to have collated many advanced Buddhist texts,

particularly the 'mental teachings' (sems-sde) of the Dzogchen. Thereafter he disseminated the translations, commentaries, and oral teachings of Guru Rinpoche and later reincarnated as a Terton.

Odran Palgyi Wangchuk

Palgyi Wangchuk, a lay disciple of Padmasambhava, received from the Great Guru many private teachings. A learned translator, he entered the Mandala of the Wrathful Tantric Deities, cutting himself free from the formation of illusory thought constructions. Through his practice of visualization, he transmuted negative and emotional obstructions and entered the stream of non-duality, immersing himself within the great river of spontaneous knowledge. His clan still preserves and practices the oral teachings of the Kama lineage.

Ma Rinchen Chok

Born into the clan of Ma in central Tibet, Rinchen Chok was trained as a monk by Śāntarakṣita and initiated into the Mantrayāna methods and practices by Guru Padmasambhava. Viewing the material world as a crystallization of thought-forms, he meditated in various caves without food and transformed rocks into edible nectar.

As a translator of Sūtras and commentaries, Rinchen Chok fully comprehended the teachings of Nāgārjuna and participated in the debate at Samye (c. 792–94) with the Chinese master Hwa-shang. He studied extensively with the great paṇḍita Vimalamitra, who instructed him in the Mahāyoga Tantras and transmitted to him all the lineages of its root text, the Guhyamūlagarbha Tantra. Recognized as one of the eight scholarly masters,[6] Rinchen Chok worked with Vimalamitra in translating this important teaching as

well as many others. During the course of his life, he wrote over 250 commentaries on the works of Padmasambhava, Vimalamitra, and Buddhaguhya, which contain the essence of the Atiyoga teachings.

After the death of Langdarma, Rinchen Chok traveled east to Kham and taught the Mahāyoga Tantras to Tsugu Rinchen Shonne who carried on his methods of explaining the tantric teachings. These have been preserved to the present time in the tradition centered in Kham known as sGyu-'phrul Khams lugs-ma. One of the most important Nyingma teachers, Ma Rinchen Chok reincarnated a number of times and rediscovered esoteric treasures of the Terma.

Lhalung Palgyi Dorje

Lhalung Palgyi Dorje was born near Lhasa at Dripkyi Karmo Rong, but moved to the eastern frontiers where he helped to protect the border between China and Tibet. Soon, overcome by sadness at the impermanence of all existence, he heard about the great Buddhist teachers at Samye and set out with his two brothers for central Tibet. There he studied with Vimalamitra and was initiated into the oral teachings of the Mantrayāna by Padmasambhava. After the Great Guru left Tibet, Palgyi Dorje wandered throughout the mountains, stopping only to meditate in various caves. One day as he was meditating on a mountain peak, a sudden wind carried him up into the sky far away to a beautiful secluded mountain. From that time on, he demonstrated extraordinary powers. Allowing his mind to rest without discursive thought, he was able to pass freely through rocks and fly from mountain to mountain wherever he wished.

Some time later, while Palgyi Dorje was meditating in a cave in central Tibet, reports of Langdarma's suppression of the Buddhists reached him and he set out to liberate the body of this mad king from the commission of further crime. Dressed in black and riding a white horse that he had covered with charcoal, Palgyi Dorje arrived in Lhasa and found the king attending a ritual dance. Joining the dancers, he awaited the right moment. With compassion, he let fly the fatal arrow, then fled, washing the charcoal from his horse in the Tsangpo River to escape detection. Continuing on to eastern Tibet, he made his home in the mountains at Tantik, where he performed sādhanas for the benefit of suffering beings. After a long life of solitude, his body became transformed into a rainbow of light, and he vanished from view.

Konchok Jungnay

Konchok Jungnay was born at Shang Taneg (North Black Horse). Given the name Langdronam, he became an influential minister under Trisong Detsen. A close disciple of Padmasambhava, he received instruction in the Dzogchen Nyingtig – the immediate experience of Being-in-itself. In deep relaxation of body and mind, he contemplated the indivisibility of appearance and nothingness – just as wind is not separate from air – and discovered within his mind the realization that is all-encompassing like the sky. With lightning and thunderbolts he directed the wrathful dagger of his clear perception to liberate both humans and non-humans from anxiety and timidity. At life's end, the body of this layman translator became an expanse of light. Through his lineage of Thaduk Dormapa, he later incarnated as the Terma master Ratna Lingpa.

Gyalwa Changchub

One of the eight self-mastering scholars of Tibet, Gyalwa Changchub received the Mantra teachings from Guru Padmasambhava and became an exemplary monk and lotsawa. Before departing from Tibet, Padmasambhava gathered together all the disciples at a place called Thaduk, or 'Multi-colored Dragon' and counseled them for twenty-one days, giving them final instructions in the practice of sādhana: ritual offerings, mantra, visualization, meditation or samādhi, and many additional spiritual exercises and techniques. At this time, Padmasambhava initiated his disciple Gyalwa Changchub into the All-encompassing Mandala, wherein Mind-as-such, birthless and undying, remains seated on the throne of unchanging Dharmakāya.

MANDĀRAVĀ

Female Disciples

Padmasambhava's inner circle also included fifteen female followers and five Ḍākinīs who incarnated as Yeshe Tsogyal, Mandāravā of Zahor, Śākyadevī of Nepal, Kālasiddhī of India, and Tashi Khyedren of Montsaog (Bhutan). In iconographic representations, Mandāravā is usually depicted to the right of Guru Rinpoche and Yeshe Tsogyal to his left.

MANDĀRAVĀ Daughter of the Zahor king, Mandāravā was regarded by everyone as an incarnate goddess. Her entire village, as well as forty royal suitors from the kingdoms of India, Persia, Turkey and China, admired her pleasing, captivating features. But thinking over her past lives, she decided to follow a spiritual path. Exercising his prescience, Padmasambhava discerned that the time had come to instruct Mandāravā and flew on a cloud from Dhanakośa Lake to

Zahor. There he found her on retreat with her followers and instructed them in the Mantrayāna teachings. The king, however, was outraged. Misunderstanding the motive for Padmasambhava's seclusion with his daughter, he decreed that she be tossed into a dark pit without sight of the sky and ordered his attendants to burn Padmasambhava at the stake. The Guru was stripped naked and his hands were tied behind his back. A rope was placed around his neck, and he was bound to a stake and wrapped in oil. He was then set aflame, and the smoke that arose hid the sun and the sky. But all the deities and Buddhas came to the Great Guru's aid. Padmasambhava transformed the pyre into a rainbow-enhaloed lake and appeared in the middle of the lake seated on the pollen bed of an enormous white lotus.

Under Guru Rinpoche's guidance, Mandāravā renounced worldly attachments and practiced meditation. On one occasion, Amitāyus appeared to them as they were meditating in a cave and placed on their heads the urn of boundless life, filled with the nectar of immortality. Thereafter Mandāravā traveled throughout the border regions of northern India and into Tibet. Never dying, she manifests in many places at different times to teach the way to liberation.

ŚĀKYADEVĪ When the queen of Nepal died in childbirth, the king abandoned his young daughter at the queen's gravesite, where she was fed and cared for by monkeys. Her hands were webbed like the feet of a duck, and her body displayed the marks of a goddess. Later, as a young woman, Śākyadevī was discovered in the cemetery by Padmasambhava and became his enlightened consort. Filled with the stream of the Guru's instruction, she alleviates sufferings that arise from fear, doubt, and worry.

KĀLASIDDHĪ Kālasiddhī was born in India into a family of weavers. When her mother died, her father, convinced that the child would not survive, carried them both to the cemetery. Mandāravā, manifesting as a tigress, came upon the child in the cemetery and, with deep compassion, fed and instructed her. Padmasambhava later initiated her into the mandala of Vajrasattva, in whom all the peaceful and wrathful deities converge and merge. Upon Padmasambhava's departure from Tibet, Kālasiddhī requested him to allow her to preserve the teachings. Thereafter she concealed many Termas throughout Nepal and Tibet, finally passing away in a mist of light.

TASHI KHYEDREN Born at Montsaog near the Nepalese border of Tibet, Tashi Khyedren was instructed by Ḍākinīs, who activated her ability to reacall past lives. Journeying to southern Tibet, she met Yeshe Tsogyal, who guided her to Guru Rinpoche. Thereafter she became the consort of his enlightening activity. Tashi Khyedren manifests as the tigress ridden by Guru Dorje Drolo, 'Changeless Comforter of All Beings'. Together they wrathfully stride over all obstacles to enlightenment, liberating sentient beings from emotional and intellectual bewilderment and revealing the all-pervasive path of the Dharma.

During his stay in Tibet, Padmasambhava also initiated fifteen female disciples who practiced the Dorje Phurbu and Chemchok sādhanas:

SHENAMZA SANGYATSO,
radiant in self-awareness, became a body of effulgent light.

SELKAR DORJE TSO
surrendered herself like a plant on a river to the stream of devotion.

TSHOMBUZA PEMA TSO,
harmonizing body, breath and mind, discovered unchanging bliss.

MALGONZA RINCHEN TSO dressed in clothes of rainbow light.

RUBZA DONDRIBMA, who subdued the twelve protectresses, was able to accomplish whatever she wished.

SHUDBUZA SHERABMA
was able to effortlessly memorize the Sūtras and śāstras.

YARAGZA CHOKYI DROMA
continues to receive praise in the heaven realms from all who study her teachings.

OCEZA KAGYALMA,
whenever in doubt, conversed with deities.

ZEMZA LHAMO,
whenever hungry, received nectar from the heavenly realms.

BARZA LHAWANGMA,
understanding the way to liberation, illumined the Dharma for others.

CHOROGZA CHANGCHUBMA
transformed herself into fire, water, and wind.

DROMA PAMTI CHENMO,
free from attachment, traveled in the sky of awareness like a bird.

RONGMANZA SHULTRIMDRON
became able to transmute rocks into sustenance.

KHAZA PALZHUNMA
liberated countless beings through the power of the phurbu.

TRUMZA SHELMAN
inspired many visions by showering flowers in celestial space.

At Chimphu near Samye, fifty-five enlightened meditators, free from desire, passed into space, their bodies vanishing like mist. At Yerpa and Shebouri, 108 meditators, free from attachments, assumed bodies as subtle as rainbows. And at Seltrag, thirty laymen and twenty-five women, free from duality, entered the radiant light of pure being. All of these, and uncounted others, were the direct disciples of the Great Guru Padmasambhava and attained enlightenment in one lifetime.

PADMASAMBHAVA AND TWENTY-FIVE DISCIPLES

Notes

1. Herukas Often depicted as wrathful deities, Herukas represent the activation of the positive qualities of mind. The eight Herukas, or tutelary deities mentioned in the biographies of the twenty-five disciples, illumine various aspects of Guru Rinpoche made manifest in meditation. Chemchok (Che-mchog) Heruka appears in the center of the mandala.

2. Hayagrīva (rTa-mgrin), the 'Horse-headed Lord', represents the wrathful manifestation of Avalokiteśvara. He is one of the tutelary deities of the maṇḍala and represents clear discernment. The Blue Annals records that "The king especially propitiated Hayagrīva. On three occasions the neighing of a horse was heard, and many people heard it." See George N. Roerich (Trans.). The Blue Annals [Deb-ther sngon-po, by 'Gos lo-tsā-ba], 2 vols., Calcutta, 1949, 1953, pp. 106–7, for a description of the eight Nyingma Tantras.

3. Vimalamitra, the chief translator of the Tantras during the early propagation of Buddhism, was a disciple of Śrī Siṃha and other great Mantrayāna masters and a major holder of the Mahāyoga and Atiyoga lineages. He is said to have been two hundred years old when he arrived in Tibet, where he translated over fifty-two volumes and various texts on the Great Dzogchen teachings (rDzogs-pa-chen-po). Some of these works are preserved in the Nyingma Gyudbum together with the profound Nyingtig instructions. Through the work of this great paṇḍita, many important Nyingma teachings were transmitted to Tibet. He attained a rainbow body and reincarnated in later times as Longchenpa and other Nyingma masters.

4. Jamyang Khyentse Wangpo (1820–92), together with Kongtrul Lodro Thaye (1813–99), were two beacons in the nineteenth-century cultural renaissance that was known as the Eclectic Movement (ris-

med) in eastern Tibet. Jamyang Khyentse collected, refined, and unified all the major spiritual lineages and traditions from among the original (rNying-ma) and new (gSar-ma) schools. His collected works total over fifty volumes and include many tantric initiations and sādhana practices.

5. The other three are Vairotsana, Kawa Paltseg, and Chokro Lui Gyaltsen.

6. These eight translator scholars are: Nyag Jñānakumāra (Yeshe Zhonnu), Kawa Paltseg, Chokro Lui Gyaltsen, Ugra Nyingpo, Vairotsana, Namkhai Nyingpo, Ma Rinchen Chok, and Nanam Yeshe De.

TSOKYI DORJE

ŚĀKYA SENGE

URGYAN DORJE CHANG

PADMASAMBHAVA

LODAN CHOGSED

PADMA GYALPO

NYIMA ODZER

DORJE DROLOD

SENGE DRADOG

PADMASAMBHAVA

Vajra Guru Mantra

PADMASAMBHAVA

O Guru, if one should rely solely on your Sādhana, which is the Vajra Guru Mantra, what benefit and advantage will come from this?

The Buddhism of Tibet is remarkable for the great variety of practices it offers to those who elect to travel the path to liberation from the sufferings of human existence. Among these various practices the use of mantra forms an important part, so much so that the Tibetan form of Buddhism is often referred to as Mantrayāna, the Mantra Vehicle.

Properly used, under competent guidance, mantra is an effective instrument for dispelling the ignorance on which our anxious lives are founded. It can lead the practitioner to a realization of the true nature of mind, for mantra is not a form of magical incantation, but rather a scientific method for bringing the mind into harmony with subtle levels of awareness and reopening avenues of communication that otherwise remain closed.

The Vajra Guru Mantra is the mantra of Guru Padmasambhava, the founder of Buddhism in Tibet. It is said to be especially beneficial for these troubled times, for it has great power to calm the tensions and anxieties so common to our age. If one sits quietly and concentrates complete attention upon the sound of one's own voice chanting the mantra, the worry and distress that keep the mind in turmoil will gradually subside, and the mind will be suffused with a deep calm.

With practice, it is possible to extend the period of peaceful concentration, thus creating a refuge from fears, doubts, and other painful mental distractions. As this serenity develops and expands, the mind gradually settles, becoming like the surface of a still pool. From this calm, awareness arises, and the self-nature of mind can be realized.

THE NINE MANIFESTATIONS OF PADMASAMBHAVA

Vajra Guru Mantra

To traverse the path, an element of faith is required. This faith is not a blind, uncritical acceptance, but an openness: a willingness to search and to discover for oneself the wisdom that has been maintained and transmitted by a continuous tradition extending back thousands of years.

Buddhism has always maintained that for those who seek within themselves, critically, persistently, and with intensity, the truth of the Dharma is self-evident. The path that leads to realization is thus a path of examination. This is true for the practice of mantra as well. The power of mantra will be revealed to those who follow the time-honored teachings with patience, sincerity, and trust.

Excerpts of an Adaptation from Tibetan

Herein is contained
the commentary of the Mystic Syllables and Benefits
of the Vajra Guru Mantra
from the gTer-ma of Sprul-sku Karma Gling-pa
a ṇa dza sa ma wa zha ma rga rma
Vajra Guru Deva Ḍākinī Hūṃ.
Homage to the Lama, the Yidam, and the Ḍakinī!
The Ḍākinī Ye-shes-mtsho-rgyal spoke:

I, Ye-shes-mtsho-rgyal, who am a mere woman, having made an offering of a vast Mandala, outer, inner, and secret, to my Guru, now make this request. O master Padmasambhava, please grant to us, we who are the people of Tibet, your unending aid and assistance in this present life and in all future lives. There has never been before, nor will there in the future ever come forth again a boon as great as yourself. I have no doubt that even I, who am a mere woman, shall be given your sādhana, which is itself a pure and precious nectar.

PADMASAMBHAVA

Vajra Guru Mantra

I see that there will come a time in the distant future when human beings will possess fickle intellects and ever-changing opinions. They will be very excitable, impatient, and excessively prone to violence. They will cling to false views regarding the holy Dharma. In particular, they will slander and belittle the doctrine of the supremely secret mantras. At that time, for all sentient beings, the three great evils of disease, poverty, and warfare with terrifying weapons will greatly increase. In particular, there will come a time of terrible suffering for Tibet and the Tibetan people. Just as ants swarm out of their nest when the nest is broken open, so troubles will swarm with great devastations across the three regions of China, Tibet, and Central Asia.

O Guru, you have proclaimed many skillful means for curing these ills. But for the people of those future times there will be no time or opportunity for the practice of sādhana. Only a very few will even have the desire to practice. On every hand disturbances and distractions will be exceedingly strong and powerful. Human beings will be unable to agree among themselves. Even the materials necessary for pūjā and the preparation for sādhana practice will be incomplete.

In such evil times, it will be extremely difficult to avert or reverse those trends. In such times as those, O Guru, if one should rely solely on your sādhana that is the Vajra Guru Mantra, what benefit and advantage will come from this? For the sake of those future beings with inferior intellects, devoid of deep spiritual understanding, please tell us.

Then the Great Master spoke:

O faithful daughter, what you have said is very true. But in such future periods of time as those, it is still certain that from practice there shall come forth benefits both immediate and ultimate for all sentient beings. I shall conceal the eighteen kinds of gTermas, such as earth-treasures, water-treasures, rock-treasures, and sky-treasures, which will contain countless numbers of sādhanas and secret teachings.

PADMASAMBHAVA AND THE GUARDIAN DEITIES OF TIBET

Vajra Guru Mantra

In those evil times, the skillful methods of those who possess good karma and the auspicious coinciding of circumstances will be exceedingly difficult to accomplish. Such times are characterized by the exhaustion of whatever merit sentient beings may possess.

Nevertheless, if at such places as the twenty four Great Places of Pilgrimage, or in the temples and villages, or on the peak of a great mountain, or on the shore of a great river, or in the uplands and lowlands inhabited by gods, demons, and ghosts. If there is one who possesses the vows of the Sangha, or even a layman of devout faith or a woman of good character, having intensively cultivated the intention to attain enlightenment, who is able to repeat the essence of the Vajra Guru Mantra one hundred times, or one thousand, or ten thousand, or one hundred thousand, or one million, or one hundred million times, or as many times as possible, the resulting power and benefits will be inconceivable to the human mind.

And in all the directions of space, the evil of disease, poverty, warfare, hostile armies, civil strive, famine, dire prophesize and ill omens shall be averted. In every direction, the good fortune of healthy cattle, abundant crops and rain in season shall come. In one's present life, in all future lives, and in the narrow difficult passage of the bardo, I shall speak to the superior person in his dreams. And it is certain that such a person, having perfected gradually the paths and the stages, shall enter into the land of Camaradvīpa as a Vidyādhara, whether male or female.

If one but repeats the mantra uninterruptedly one hundred times a day, he will appear in the thoughts of others in favorable fashion, there will come to him effortlessly abundant food, wealth, and good fortune. If one repeats the mantra as often as one thousand times or ten thousand times and so on, he shall gain control over the minds of others, and it is certain that he shall attain power and blessing.

If one repeats the mantra one hundred thousand or ten million times or more, he will accumulate all the power of the three worlds and gain control over the three realms of existence. Gods and demons shall

PADMASAMBHAVA

become his servants, and he shall attain without any impediment whatsoever the Four Magical Rights. Then he will be able to help immeasurably all sentient beings as much as he desires. If one is able to count as many as thirty million or seventy million, then all the Buddhas of the three times of past, present, and future shall always be with him. Indeed, he shall be identical with me. All the gods, rakṣasas, and fearsome mountain deities shall promise to listen to his commands and obey him, accomplishing whatever he entrust to them.

The superior person will in this very life attain the rainbow body. The intermediate person will on the occasion of the Chikhai bardo realize the clear light of self illumination ('od-gsal). Even the inferior person, once having seen my face in the bardo, will be delivered from the arising of the (expected) appearances, and having been reborn in Camaradvīpa, he shall give immeasurable aid to all sentient beings.

Then the Ḍākinī Ye-shes-mtsho-rgyal further requested:

O Great Master, we thank you for such a great boon of vast and immeasurable power and benefit. But for the sake of future sentient beings, please expound briefly in sutra fashion on the immeasurable power and benefit of the commentary on the mystic syllables of the mantra of Guru Padma.

Then the Great Master spoke:

O daughter of a noble family, that which is called the Vajra Guru Mantra is not only my name, but it also represents the very heart of the vital essence of the Yidams, the four types of Tantras, the Nine Vehicles and the eighty-four thousand sections of the Dharma. This capital mantra is complete and perfect, for it is the very essence of all the Buddhas of the three times, of all the Gurus, Devatas, Ḍākinīs, and Dharmapālas.

If one should ask what marks the cause of this perfection, then let him listen well and fix it firmly in his mind. Let him repeat the

PADMASAMBHAVA

mantra again and again. Let him write it down. Then let him instruct and explain its meaning to all sentient beings of future ages.

Explanation of the Mantra

OṂ AḤ HŪṂ VAJRA GURU PADMA SIDDHI HŪṂ

As for OṂ, AḤ and HŪṂ, they are the supreme essence of the Body, Speech and Mind. Vajra is the supreme essence of the Vajra family. Guru is the supreme essence of the Ratna family. Padma is the supreme essence of the Padma family. Siddhi is the supreme essence of the Karma family. As for HŪṂ, it is the supreme essence of the Tathāgata family.

OṂ AḤ HŪṂ VAJRA GURU PADMA SIDDHI HŪṂ

As for OṂ, it is the perfection of the Sambhogakāya which embodies the Buddhas of the five families. AḤ is the perfection complete and unchanging of the Dharmakāya. HŪṂ is the perfection of the Guru, who is the Nirmaṇakāya, in the space before one. Vajra is the perfection of the divine assembly of Herukas. Guru is the perfection of the divine assembly of Guru Vidyādharas. Padma is the perfection of the divine assembly of Ḍākas and Ḍākinīs. Siddhi is the vital energy of all the Wealth goods and Treasure Lords. HŪṂ is the vital energy of all the Dharmapālas, without exception.

OṂ AḤ HŪṂ VAJRA GURU PADMA SIDDHI HŪṂ

As for OṂ, AḤ and HŪṂ, they are the vital energies of the three types of Tantras (Father, Mother, and Non-dual). Vajra is the vital energy of the two sections called the Vinaya and the Sūtras. Guru is the vital energy of the sections Abhidharma and Caryā Tantra. Padma is the vital energy of the two called Upāya Tantra and Yoga Tantra. Siddhi is the vital energy of the two called Mahā Yoga and Anu Yoga. HŪṂ is the vital energy of the Ati Yoga.

OṂ AḤ HŪṂ VAJRA GURU PADMA SIDDHI HŪṂ

By OṂ, AḤ and HŪṂ, all obscurations that derive from the three

PADMASAMBHAVA

poisons will be purified. By Vajra, all obscurations that derive from hatred will be purified. By Guru, all obscurations that derive from pride will be purified. By Padma, all obscurations that derive from greed will be purified. By Siddhi, all obscurations that derive from envy will be purified. By HŪṂ, all obscurations that derive from all forms of emotionality will be purified.

OṂ AḤ HŪṂ VAJRA GURU PADMA SIDDHI HŪṂ

By OṂ, AḤ and HŪṂ, one will attain the Dharmakāya, Sambhogakāya and Nirmaṇakāya. By Vajra, one will obtain the Mirror-like wisdom. By Guru, one will obtain the Wisdom of Sameness. By Padma, one will obtain the Discriminating Wisdom. By Siddhi, one will obtain the All-Accomplishing Wisdom. By HŪṂ, one will perfectly obtain all that derives from Wisdom.

OṂ AḤ HŪṂ VAJRA GURU PADMA SIDDHI HŪṂ

By OṂ, AḤ and HŪṂ, one will control gods, demons, and men. By Vajra, one will control such hostile spirits as gandharvas and fire spirits. By guru, one will control such hostile spirits as Yama and rakṣasas. By Padma, one will control such hostile spirits as water sprites and air spirits. By Siddhi, one will control such hostile spirits as yakṣas and powerful demons. By HŪṂ one will control such hostile spirits as planetary genii and earth lords.

OṂ AḤ HŪṂ VAJRA GURU PADMA SIDDHI HŪṂ

By OṂ, AḤ and HŪṂ one will obtain the six perfections. By Vajra one will realize all the magical rites that are peaceful. By Guru one will realize all the magical rites that increase prosperity. By Padma one will realize all the magical rites of overpowering enchantment. By Siddhi one will realize all the magical rites of worldly success. By HŪṂ one will realize all the magical rites that are terrifying.

OṂ AḤ HŪṂ VAJRA GURU PADMA SIDDHI HŪṂ

By OṂ, AḤ and HŪṂ one will counteract the magical influences of both Lamas and Bonpos. By Vajra one will counteract the hostile influences of the nemesis of the gods. By Guru one will counteract the hostile influences of gods, rakṣasas, and nature deities. By Padma

PADMASAMBHAVA WITH EIGHT MANIFESTATIONS AND LINEAGE MASTERS

one will counteract the hostile influences of minor worldly deities and demons. By Siddhi one will counteract the hostile influences of nāgas and earth-lords. By HŪṂ one will counteract all the hostile influences of gods, demons, and men.

OṂ AḤ HŪṂ VAJRA GURU PADMA SIDDHI HŪṂ

By OṂ, AḤ and HŪṂ one will vanquish the militant hosts of the five poisons. Vajra will vanquish the militant hosts born of hatred. Guru will vanquish the militant hosts born of pride. Padma will vanquish the militant hosts born of greed. Siddhi will vanquish the militant hosts born of envy. By HŪṂ one will vanquish the militant hosts of gods, demons, and men.

OṂ AḤ HŪṂ VAJRA GURU PADMA SIDDHI HŪṂ

By OṂ, AḤ and HŪṂ one will obtain the siddhis of body, speech, and mind. By Vajra one will obtain the siddhis of the peaceful and wrathful deities. By Guru one will obtain the siddhis of the Vidyādhara Guru. By Padma one will obtain the siddhis of the Ḍākinīs and Dharmapālas. By Siddhi one will obtain the siddhis both ordinary and supreme. By HŪṂ one will obtain all of the conceivable siddhis.

OṂ AḤ HŪṂ VAJRA GURU PADMA SIDDHI HŪṂ

By OṂ, AḤ and HŪṂ one will be reborn in the Primordial Realm. By Vajra one will be reborn in the Realm of Manifest Happiness, in the eastern direction. By Guru one will be reborn in the Fortunate Realm, in the southern direction. By Padma one will be reborn in the Realm of Great Bliss, in the western direction. By Siddhi one will be reborn in the Realm of Infinite Peace, in the northern direction. By HŪṂ one will be reborn in the Realm of Emptiness, in the center.

TSOKYI DORJE

URGYAN DORJE CHANG

ŚĀKYA SENGE

PADMASAMBHAVA

PADMA GYALPO

LODAN CHOGSED

NYIMA ODZER

DORJE DROLOD

SENGE DRADOG

PADMASAMBHAVA WITH MANDARAVA AND YESHE TSOGYAL

Prayers

PADMASAMBHAVA

ཚིག་བདུན་གསོལ་འདེབས།

tsig dun sol deb

Seven Line Prayer

ཧཱུྃ༔

hūṃ

ཨོ་རྒྱན་ཡུལ་གྱི་ནུབ་བྱང་མཚམས།།

orgyen yul gyi nub chang tsam

In the northwestern land of Oḍḍiyāna

པདྨ་གེ་སར་སྡོང་པོ་ལ།།

pema ge sar dong po la

born in the pistil of a lotus blossom

ཡ་མཚན་མཆོག་གི་དངོས་གྲུབ་བརྙེས།།

yatsen chog gi ngo drup nyey

endowed with the most wondrous

spiritual realization,

པདྨ་འབྱུང་གནས་ཞེས་སུ་གྲགས།།

pema jung nay zhey su drag

you are renowned as the

Lotus-born Padmasambhava

འཁོར་དུ་མཁའ་འགྲོ་མང་པོས་བསྐོར།།

kor du khan dro mang po kor

surrounded by hosts of ḍākinīs

NINE MANIFESTATIONS OF PADMASAMBHAVA WITH ABBOT AND KING

ཁྱེད་ཀྱི་རྗེས་སུ་བདག་བསྒྲུབ་ཀྱི།།

kyed kyi jey su dag drup kyi

following you I shall practice.

བྱིན་གྱིས་རློབ་ཕྱིར་གཤེགས་སུ་གསོལ།།

shin gi lob chir sheg su sol

Please come bestow your blessings.

གུ་རུ་པདྨ་སི་དྡྷི་ཧཱུྃ།།

guru pema siddhi hūṃ

Guru Padma Siddhi Hūṃ

PADMASAMBHAVA

Prayer to Orgyen Rinpoche

ཨོ་རྒྱན་རིན་པོ་ཆེ་ལ་གསོལ་བ་འདེབས།།
orgyen rin po che la sol wa deb
Orgyen Rinpoche I pray to you.

འགལ་རྐྱེན་བར་ཆད་མི་འབྱུང་ཞིང་།།
gal kyen bar chad mi jung zhing
May adverse conditions not arise,

མཐུན་རྐྱེན་བསམ་པ་འགྲུབ་པ་དང་།།
tun kyen sam pa drub pa dang
and favorable ones bring about my heart's desires.

མཆོག་དང་ཐུན་མོང་དངོས་གྲུབ་སྩོལ།།
chok dang thun mong ngo drub tsol
Please grant the supreme and common siddhis!

འཇམ་དབྱངས་མཁྱེན་བརྩེའི་དབང་པོས་གསུང་།།

Composed by Jamyang Khyentse Wangpo

PADMASAMBHAVA

Prayer to Padmasambhava

ཨེ་མ་ཧོ།

དཀོན་མཆོག་རྩ་གསུམ་བདེ་གཤེགས་ཀུན་འདུས་དཔལ།།

e ma ho!
kon chog tsa sum de sheg kun du pahl
How amazing! You embody the Three Jewels,
the Three Roots,
and all the Sugatas in your glory.

སྙིགས་དུས་འགྲོ་བ་མགོན་མེད་སྐྱབས་གཅིག་པུ།།

nyig du dro wa gon med kyab chig pu
You are the sole refuge of unprotected beings
in this dark age.

ཐུགས་རྗེ་གློག་ལྟར་མྱུར་བའི་ཐོད་ཕྲེང་རྩལ།།

tuk jey log tar nyur wey tod treng tsal
Your compassion is as swift as lightning, Tod Treng Tsal.

མ་ཧཱ་གུ་རུ་པདྨ་ཧེ་རུ་ཀཿ

ma ha gu ru pad ma he ru ka
Great Guru Padma Heruka,

མོས་གུས་གདུང་ཤུགས་དྲག་པོས་གསོལ་བ་འདེབས།།

mo gu dung shug drag po sol wa deb
with intense longing and fervent devotion,
I pray to you.

PADMASAMBHAVA WITH THE ABBOT ŚĀNTARAKṢITA AND KING TRISONG DETSEN

དགྲ་གདོན་བགེགས་དང་བར་ཆད་བྱད་ཕུར་བཟློག།

dra don geg dang bar chad jad pur dog

Turn back enemies, demons, obstructors,
obstacles,and spells.

མ་རུང་རྒྱལ་བསེན་འབྱུང་པོ་དམ་ལ་ཐོགས།།

ma rung gyel sen jung po dam la tog

Bind by sacred oath all hostile spirits and jungpo demons,

བསམ་པ་ལྷུན་གྱིས་འགྲུབ་པར་བྱིན་གྱིས་རློབས།།

sam pa lhun gyi drup par shin gyi lob

and grant your blessings so that our wishes
may be perfectly fulfilled.

མདོ་མཁྱེན་བརྩེ་ཡེ་ཤེས་རྡོ་རྗེས་གསུངས་སོ།།

Composed by Do Khyentse Yeshe Dorje

PADMASAMBHAVA WITH LINEAGE MASTERS AND DHARMA PROTECTORS

Prayer to Guru Rinpoche

སྐྱབས་གནས་ཀུན་འདུས་ཀྱི་ངོ་བོ།།
kyab ney kun du kyi ngo bo
Essence of all the sources of refuge,

མཁྱེན་བརྩེ་ནུས་པའི་བདག་ཉིད།།
kyen tsey nu pey dag nyid
embodiment of enlightened knowledge,
love, and power,

དྲིན་ཅན་མཚོ་སྐྱེས་རྡོ་རྗེ།།
drin chen tso kyey dor jey
most kind Lake-born Vajra,

སྙིང་ནས་གསོལ་བ་འདེབས་སོ།།
nying nay sol wa deb so
from the depths of my heart, I pray to you.

རྟག་ཏུ་དབྱེར་མེད་ཐུགས་རྗེས།།
tag tu yer med tug jey
Hold me forever inseparable from you
through your compassion,

བདག་རྒྱུད་བྱིན་གྱིས་རློབས་ཤིག།
dag gyud shin gyi lob shig
and bestow your blessings upon my mindstream.

དཔལ་སྤྲུལ་རིན་པོ་ཆེས་མཛད་པ།

Composed by Patrul Rinpoche

MINDROLING PADMA MURAL

དུས་གསུམ་སངས་རྒྱས།

Du sum sang gyey

Prayer to Guru Rinpoche, Buddha of the Three Times

དུས་གསུམ་སངས་རྒྱས་གུ་རུ་རིན་པོ་ཆེ།།

du sum sang gyey gu ru rin po che

Buddha of the Three Times, Guru Rinpoche,

དངོས་གྲུབ་ཀུན་བདག་བདེ་བ་ཆེན་པོའི་ཞབས།།

ngo drub kun dag dey wa chen poi zhab

lord of all spiritual accomplishments, great blissful one,

བར་ཆད་ཀུན་སེལ་བདུད་འདུལ་དྲག་པོ་རྩལ།།

bar ched kun sel dud dul drag po tsahl

dispeller of all obstacles, wrathful tamer of demon Maras,

གསོལ་བ་འདེབས་སོ་བྱིན་གྱིས་རླབས་ཏུ་གསོལ།།

sol wa deb so shin gyi lab tu sol

pray, grant your blessings that

ཕྱི་ནང་གསང་བའི་བར་ཆད་ཞི་བ་དང་།།

chi nang sang wey bar chad zhi wa dang

pacify outer, inner, and secret obstacles.

བསམ་པ་ལྷུན་གྱིས་འགྲུབ་པར་བྱིན་གྱིས་རློབས།།

sam pa lhun gyi drup par shin gyi lob

Grant your blessings so that our deepest wishes

are perfectly fulfilled.

PADMASAMBHAVA

Prayer to the Mahapandita

རྒྱ་གར་པཎ་ཆེན་བོད་ལ་བཀའ་དྲིན་ཆེ།།
gya gar pan chen bod la ka drin chey
Mahapandita of India, so gracious to Tibet,

པདྨ་འབྱུང་གནས་སྐུ་ལ་འདས་འཁྲུངས་མེད།།
pema jung nay ku la day trung med
Lotus-born One, embodied without birth or death,

ད་ལྟ་ལྷོ་ནུབ་སྲིན་པོའི་ཁ་གནོན་མཛད།།
da ta lho nub srin poi kha non dzed
today you must go tame the demons of the Southwest.

ཨོ་རྒྱན་རིན་པོ་ཆེ་ལ་གསོལ་བ་འདེབས།།
orgyen rin po che la solwa deb
Orgyan Rinpoche, to you we pray.

PADMASAMBHAVA

བསམ་པ་མྱུར་འགྲུབ།

Sam pa nyur drup

Swiftly Answer Our Prayers

ཨེ་མ་ཧོ།

E ma ho!

How amazing!

མཚོ་དབུས་གེ་སར་པདྨའི་སྡོང་པོ་ལ།།

tso u ge sar padma dong po la

In the center of the lake, within the pistil of a lotus,

སྐུ་ལྔ་ཡེ་ཤེས་ལྷུན་གྱིས་གྲུབ་པའི་ལྷ།།

ku nga ye shey lhun gyi drup pey lha

Lord of the perfect wisdom of the five kayas,

རང་བྱུང་ཆེན་པོ་པདྨ་ཡབ་ཡུམ་ནི།།

rang jung chen po padma yab yum ni

Great Self-arisen One, Padma with your consort,

མཁའ་འགྲོའི་སྤྲིན་ཕུང་འཁྲིགས་ལ་གསོལ་བ་འདེབས།།

kan dro trin pung trig la sol wa deb

encircled by billowing clouds of dakinis, to you we pray:

བསམ་པ་མྱུར་དུ་འགྲུབ་པར་བྱིན་གྱིས་རློབས།།

sam pa nyur du drup par shin gyi lob

grant your blessings so that our wishes

may be swiftly fulfilled.

PADMASAMBHAVA

ལས་ངན་སྤྱད་པའི་རྣམ་སྨིན་མཐུས་བསྐྱེད་པའི།།
ley ngen shed pey nam min tu kyed pey
Through the force of the ripening of negative karma,

ནད་གདོན་བར་གཅོད་དམག་འཁྲུག་མུ་གེའི་ཚོགས།།
ned don bar chod mag trug mu gey tsog
all disease, evil forces, obstacles, wars,
and famine come forth.

ཁྱོད་ཞལ་དྲན་པའི་མོད་ལ་ཟད་བྱེད་པའི།།
kyod zhal dren pey mod la zed jed pey
Recalling your face for an instant
will exhaust this karma:

ཞལ་བཞེས་སྙིང་ནས་བསྐུལ་ལོ་ཨོ་རྒྱན་རྗེ།།
zhal zhey nying ney ku lo orgyan je
this sacred promise we invoke from the depths
of our hearts, Oddiyana Lord.

བསམ་པ་མྱུར་དུ་འགྲུབ་པར་བྱིན་གྱིས་རློབས།།
sam pa nyur du drup par shin gyi lob
Grant your blessings so that our wishes
may be swiftly fulfilled.

དད་དང་ཚུལ་ཁྲིམས་གཏོང་ལ་སྒོམས་པ་དང་།།
ded dang tsul trim tong la gom pa dang
Practicing faith, morality, and generosity,

NINE MANIFESTATIONS, DHARMA PROTECTORS, AND LINEAGE MASTERS

ཐོས་པས་རྒྱུད་གྲོལ་ཁྲེལ་ཡོད་ངོ་ཚ་ཤེས།།
tu pey gyu drol trel yod ngo tsa shey
liberating the mind through listening to Dharma,
self-respect, propriety,

ཤེས་རབ་ཕུན་སུམ་ཚོགས་པའི་ནོར་བདུན་པོ།།
shey rab pun sum tsog pey nor dun po
and perfect wisdom. May these Seven Riches

སེམས་ཅན་ཀུན་གྱི་རྒྱུད་ལ་རང་ཞུགས་ནས།།
sem chen kun gyi gyu la rang zhug ney
arise, uncaused, in the minds of us all,

འཇིག་རྟེན་བདེ་སྐྱིད་ལྡན་པར་དབུགས་འབྱིན་མཛོད།།
jig ten dey kyid den par woo jin zod
restoring the well-being and happiness of the world.

བསམ་པ་མྱུར་དུ་འགྲུབ་པར་བྱིན་གྱིས་རློབས།།
sam pa nyur du drup par shin gyi lob
Grant your blessings so that our wishes
may be swiftly fulfilled.

གང་ལ་ནད་དང་སྡུག་བསྔལ་མི་འདོད་རྐྱེན།།
gang la ned dang dug ngel mi do kyen
When sick or suffering from unwanted conditions,

NINE MANIFESTATIONS, DHARMA PROTECTORS, AND LINEAGE MASTERS

འབྱུང་པོའི་གདོན་དང་རྒྱལ་པོའི་ཆད་པ་དང་།།
jung poi don dang gyel poi ched pa dang
under demonic possession or tyrannic rule,

མེ་ཆུ་གཅན་གཟན་ལམ་འཕྲང་འཇིགས་པ་ཆེ།།
mey chu chen zen lam trang jig pa che
stricken by great fear due to fires, floods,
treacherous paths, or attack by wild beasts,

ཚེ་ཡི་ཕ་མཐར་གཏུགས་པའི་གནས་སྐབས་ཀུན།།
tsey yi pa tar tug pey ney kab kun
and when the end of life is reached,
in all these situations,

སྐྱབས་དང་རེ་ས་གཞན་དུ་མ་མཆིས་པས།།
kyab dang rey sa zhen du ma chi pey
our only refuge and hope is you, we have no other.

ཐུགས་རྗེས་ཟུང་ཞིག་གུ་རུ་ཨོ་རྒྱན་རྗེ།།
tuk jey zung zhig gu ru orgyen jey
With your compassion, hold us close, Oddiyana Lord.

བསམ་པ་མྱུར་དུ་འགྲུབ་པར་བྱིན་གྱིས་རློབས།།
sam pa nyur du drup par shin gyi lob
Grant your blessings so that our wishes
may be swiftly fulfilled.

PADMA JUNGNEY

URGYAN DORJE CHANG

ŚĀKYA SENGE

PADMASAMBHAVA

PADMA GYALPO

LODAN CHOGSED

NYIMA ODZER

DORJE DROLOD

SENGE DRADOG

THE COPPER MOUNTAIN MANDALA OF PADMASAMBHAVA

URGYAN DORJE CHANG

ŚĀKYA SENGE

PADMASAMBHAVA

PADMA GYALPO

LODAN CHOGSED

NYIMA ODZER

DORJE DROLOD

SENGE DRADOG

PADMASAMBHAVA WITH CONSORT

PADMASAMBHAVA

CONTINUUM OF ENLIGHTENMENT: THE GREAT GURU WITH AMITĀBHA AND ŚĀKYAMUNI

PADMASAMBHAVA ATTENDED BY YESHE TSOGYAL AND MANDARAVA

Index

Index

A

Abhidharma 163, 211

AH 211-215

Amitābha 49-51, 58, 60, 66, 71, 77-78, 82, 139, 152

Amitāyus 60, 85, 182

Amoghasiddhi 139

Ānanda 53, 59, 81, 121

Arūpadhātu 121

Atiyoga 81, 107, 148, 156, 176, 186

Avalokiteśvara 49-50, 60, 66, 71, 77-78, 87-88, 186

B

Bandhe 161, 163

Barza Lhawangma 184

Bhagavan 50

Bhikṣu 106

Bodh Gayā 66, 79, 81, 121

Bodhisattva 52, 58-71, 77, 81-82, 87-89, 105, 111, 120, 142-144, 152

body 211-215

Bonpo 89, 109, 143-144, 154, 169, 172, 213

Buddha 49-60, 65-66, 71-74, 77-78, 81-82, 85-91, 105-107, 110, 119-121, 137-138, 142, 144, 148-149, 153, 176, 182, 209-211

 of the five families 211-215

 of the Ten Directions 51-53, 58-59, 71

 of the Three Times 49, 73, 89, 209

 second 71

 Śākyamuni 71

Buddhadharma 87-88, 119, 144

Buddhaguhya 81, 121, 176

Buddhahood 52, 57, 72-74, 120

Buddhism 71-72, 123, 137-144, 151, 166, 186, 201-203

C

Citta 51, 58

Chemchok Sādhana 183

Chimed Padma Jung 61

Chimphu 117, 119, 137, 169, 184

Chorogza Changchubma 184

compassion 49-50, 71, 77, 87, 111, 120, 139, 146-147, 178, 182

Copper-colored Mountain 120, 147

cremation grounds 79

D

Ḍākinī 52-66, 79-82, 92-97, 120-121, 154, 161, 181-183, 203, 209-211, 215

Danma Tsemang 165

Dechen Lingpa 157

deed 55-57, 64, 72, 94, 110

deity 79, 82, 101, 115, 117, 120, 139-140, 143, 150, 174, 184, 186, 209-215

 tutelary 139, 186

 peaceful and wrathful 81, 182, 215

Dhanakośa, Lake 51-52, 61, 77, 181

Index

Dharmakāya 49-51, 73, 180, 211-213
Dharma 49-66, 72-73, 83, 86-88, 93-94, 106-116, 119, 123, 137, 144, 163, 183-184, 203-205, 209
  Wheel 50, 57
Diamond Path 73, 137
Diamond Throne 89, 91
disciples – twenty-five 137-141, 186
dispeller of darkness 72
Do Khyentse Yeshe Dorje 237
doctrine 62, 78, 81, 85-91, 105-113, 145, 148, 205
Dorje Chang 61
Dorje Dragpo Tsal 55, 61, 79
Dorje Drolod 72, 85, 183
Dorje Dudjom 89, 95, 159
Dorje Phurbu – see Vajrakīla
  Sādhana 183
Droma Pamti Chenmo 184
Du sum sang gyey 241
Dzogchen 121, 145, 173, 186
  Nyingtig 179
Dzogpa Chenpo 54, 60

E
Eight Great Cemeteries 53
Eight Manifestations of the Guru 53
eighty-four thousand sections of the Dharma 209
emotionality 213
empowerments 53, 59-60, 79, 82
enchantment 213
enlightenment 57, 79, 121, 138-140, 147, 183-184, 207
envy 213
Excellent Ones, Two 54, 61

F
faith 54-59, 63-66, 91-94, 110, 149, 171, 203, 207
Four Magical Rights 209

G
Ghandarva 100, 103
Garab Dorje 54, 81, 121
Gesar 158
Great Guru 71-72, 74, 91, 137, 164, 174, 177, 182, 184, 237
Great Places of Pilgrimage 207
Great Seal 113
greed 213
gTer-ma see Terma
Guhyamūlagarbha Tantra 175
Guru 49, 53, 55, 63, 71, 73, 81, 83-86
Guru's Mind 74, 119, 122, 161
Gu-ru'i-rnam-thar 57
Guru Rinpoche 72-73, 117, 139, 145-151, 158, 161, 164, 173, 181-183, 186, 240-241
Guru Śākya Senge 59
Guṇa 51, 58
Gyalwa Changchub 144, 180
Gyalwa Choyang 152, 156
Gyalway Lodro 144, 170

H
hatred 213
Hayagrīva 60, 63, 81, 139, 143, 149, 152, 186
Heruka 53, 79-81, 117, 139-142, 149-159, 170, 186, 211, 237
  Chemchok 142
  Dragnag 149
  Lhamed 157

Teachings, Eight 53
Wrathful 150
Yadak 153-154
Yangdag 170
Hīnayāna 116
HRĪ 51, 58, 77
HŪM 81, 211-215, 229
human existence 72, 201
Hūmkāra 153, 170
Hwashang 175

I
ignorance 162, 201
Indrabhūti 58, 61, 77-78

J
Jambudvīpa 49, 55
Jamyang Khyentse Wangpo 160, 186, 233
Jigten Chodto 158-159
Jñānakāya 52

K
Kadu 62
Kālasiddhī 181-183
Kama 174
Kāmadhātu 121
Karchen Palgyi Wangchuk 154
karma 51, 58, 93, 157, 203, 207
Family 211-215
Kawa Paltseg 95, 141, 144, 166, 187
Kāya 51, 58, 73
Khaza Palzhunma 184
Khye'u Chung Lotsawa 171
King Ralpachen 88
klong-sde 149
Konchok Jungnay 179

L
Lakṣaṇayāna 53
lama 49, 66, 106, 157, 203, 213
Land of Snow 55, 65, 88
Langdarma 151, 176-178
Lhalung Palgyi Dorje 177
Loden Chogsed Tsal 61, 82
Longchenpa 163, 186
Lord of Mystic Power 88-89
Lord of Wisdom 87
lotsāwa 91, 116, 158, 166, 171, 180
Lotus Born 49, 61, 77, 78, 83, 119, 137, 229, 236

M
Mahāpaṇḍita 166, 171, 243
Ma Rinchen Chok 141, 144, 175-176, 187
Māra 101, 113, 244
Mahākāla 82
Mahāmudrā 60
Mahāsiddha 170
Mahāyāna 82, 116, 142, 151
Mahāyoga 186,
Tantras 81, 175-176
Malgonza Rinchen Tso 183
man-ngag-gi-sde 149
Mandala 51, 62, 66, 73, 81, 85, 92, 100, 117, 137-138, 142-143, 146, 150, 152-159, 174, 180, 186, 203
Unity 82, 142
Mandāravā 61, 83-85, 181-182
Mañjuśrī 49, 87-88, 145, 150
Mañjuśrīmitra 53, 60
Mantra 54, 66, 106, 116, 120, 139, 151, 164, 180

Mantrayāna 55, 59, 65, 83, 85, 119, 142, 144, 149-151, 153, 155, 160, 169-172, 175, 177, 182, 186
Secret 51, 60, 82
Inner and Outer 53, 61, 78
mental distractions 201
mind 201-215
Nature of 170, 201
Monlam Chenmo 66
Mudrā 99, 164, 169-172

N
nāga 54, 58, 61, 77-78, 99, 103, 115, 215
Nāgārjuna 175
Nāgārjunagarbha 60
Nālandā 71, 86
Namkhai Nyingpo 119, 144, 153-154, 187
Nanam Phurbu lineage 163
Ngakpa 151
Nine Heart Sons 56, 63
Nine Yānas 54
Nirmaṇakāya 49-50, 53, 73
Non-Returners 54
Nyima Odzer 82
Nyingma 65, 123, 137, 141, 149, 155, 156-157, 163, 167, 176
Gyudbum see Nyingma Tantras
Tantras 141, 151, 157, 163, 186
Nyingmapa 122, 164
Nyingtig 149, 179, 186

O
obscuration 211, 213
Oceza Kagyalma 184
Oḍḍiyāna 49, 51-52, 58, 61, 77, 121
Odran Palgyi Wangchuk 174
OM 211-215
Orgyen Kandro Ling Chenmo 58
Orgyen Rinpoche 233
Ornaments, Six 54, 61

P
Palchenpo 63
Palgyi Yeshe 157
Palgyi Senge 89, 144, 158
Shudbu 168-169
Padma – family 211-215
Gyalpo 78
Gyelpo 62
Jung 61, 66
Jungnay 78, 106
Tod Treng Tsal 54
Parinirvāṇa 51
Sutra 50
Patrul Rinpoche 238
peaceful 201, 213
Perfection 73, 209-211
Great 114, 121
Six 213
phur-bu 72, 150
poison
five 109, 215
three 213
Prabhahasti 52, 59, 61
Prabhāvatī 61
Prajñāpāramitā 163
prayers 227
pride 189
prosperity 213
purification 211-215

R
rainbow body 58, 63, 186, 209

Ratna
family 211-215
Lingpa 179
Realm
Fortunate 215
of Emptiness 215
of Great Bliss 215
of Infinite Bliss 215
of Manifest Happiness 215
Primordial 215
refuge 65, 73, 201, 231, 233, 239
Rewalsar, Lake 121
Rigzin Goddem 160
Rigdzin Śrī Siṃha 54, 60
Rongmanza Shultrimdron 184
Rubza Dondribma 183
Rūpadhātu 121

S
sādhana 53, 60, 79, 117, 137, 139, 143, 149-151, 154, 158-159, 162-165, 178, 180, 183, 187, 201-205
Sākyadevī 93, 181-182
Sam pa nyur drup 235
Sambhogakāya 49-50, 73, 211-215
saṃsāra 78, 107, 117, 139
Sangha 207
Śāntarakṣita, Abbot 61, 88-89, 116, 142-144, 148, 152, 155, 159, 166 175
Sattmas 52, 58
Samantabhadra 49-50
Samye 55, 63, 88, 95, 114-121, 137, 143, 150, 155, 159, 166, 169, 175-177, 184
Sangye Yeshe 147, 150-151
Selkar Dorje Tso 183
Seltrag 184
sems-sde 149, 173
Senge Dradrog 55, 62
Seven Line Prayer 229
Shebouri 184
Shenamza Sangyatso 183
Shudbuza Sherabma 183
Siddha 54-56, 61, 63, 79, 89, 150, 153
siddhis 53, 61, 147, 168, 215, 231
skillful means 52, 205
Songtsen Gampo 88, 145
Sogpo Lhapal 144, 161-162
speech 211-215
Sprul-sku Karma Gling-pa 203
Śrī Siṃha 81, 121, 148, 186
Sukhāvatī 49, 57, 77
Sūtra 54, 59, 66, 81, 114-116, 137, 140-145, 151, 155, 165, 175, 183, 209-211
Parinirvāṇa 50
of Predictions in Magadha 51

T
Tantra 51, 53, 72, 81-82, 114-116, 137, 141-143, 151, 157, 163-165, 175-176, 186, 209
Caryā 211
Father, Mother and Non-dual 211
Mamo 168
Phurbu 168
section 53, 60
Shinje 168
Upāya 211
Yoga 211
Tashi Khyedren 181-183
Tathāgata
family 211-215
Ten Directions 51, 71, 73

Tenpa Namkha 172
Terchen Duddul Dorje Lingpa 171
Terma 119, 122, 147, 160-161, 165, 171, 176, 179, 183, 205
Thaduk Dormapa 179
Three Times 71, 109
Three Yogas 81
Thorchog Chen 61
Three Kāyas see Trikāya
Tibet 55-66, 71-72, 92-95, 104-105, 114-116, 119-122, 137, 142-152, 159, 164-183, 186-187, 201-205, 235
Tod Treng 53, 231
treasure 57, 64, 91-104, 119, 122, 147, 167, 170, 176
  Earth 205
  Water 205
  Rock 205
  Sky 205
Trikāya 49, 73
  Lama 66
Tripiṭaka 82, 116
Trisong Detsen 55, 88-91, 95, 105, 115, 117, 137, 142-148, 152, 158-159, 168, 170, 179
troubled times 201
Trumza Shelman 184
Tshombuza Pema Tso 183
tsig dun sol deb 229
Tsokyi
  Dorje 52
  Gyalwa 65

V
Vaca 51, 58
Vairotsana 116-119, 141-144, 148-149, 155, 187
Vajra 51, 54, 61, 97-98
  Asana 50, 55, 62
  family 211-215
  Garuḍa 86
  Vārāhī 54, 61
Vajra Guru Mantra 199-215
Vajradhara 49-50, 121
Vajrakīla 61, 87, 139, 146, 149-151, 155, 159, 162-163, 169
Vajrapāṇi 87-88
Vajrasattva 182
Vajrayāna 60, 71, 82, 116, 137, 141
Vehicle 50, 106, 201, 209
  Causal 49
  Nine 209
Vidyāmantra Dhara 49
Vidyādhara 53, 56, 60-62, 207, 211, 215
  Eight 60
Vimalamitra 116, 143, 149, 155, 175-177, 186
Vinaya 166, 211

W
Wangpo De 59
Wisdom
  all-accomplishing 213
  Discriminating 213
  Mirror-like 213
  of Sameness 213
Wish-fulfilling Gem 49, 77-78
worldly success 213
wrathful 72, 79, 81, 85-89, 115,117, 120, 139, 143, 150, 179, 182, 186, 215, 229
  tantric deities 174

Y
Yakṣas 213
Yama 213
Yamāntaka 150
Yaragza Chokyi Droma 184
Yerpa 184
ye-shes 122, 146, 203, 209
Ye-shes-mtsho-rgyal 203, 209
Yeshe Dorje 66, 237
Yeshe Tsogyal 117, 122, 146-147, 151, 164, 181-183
Yeshe De 141, 163, 187
Yeshe Yang 161
Yeshe Zhonnu 155-156, 162, 187
Yidam 203, 209

Z
Zemza Lhamo 184

མི་མཐུན་པའི་ཕྱོགས་
ཐམས་ཅད་ལས་རྣམ་པར་རྒྱལ་ཞིང་
བཀྲ་ཤིས་པར་གྱུར་ཅིག

མི་མཐུན་
པའི་ཕྱོགས་
ཐམས་ཅད་
ལས་རྣམ་པར་
རྒྱལ་ཞིང་
བཀྲ་ཤིས་
པར་གྱུར་ཅིག

མི་མཐུན་
པའི་ཕྱོགས་
ཐམས་ཅད་
ལས་རྣམ་པར་
རྒྱལ་ཞིང་
བཀྲ་ཤིས་
པར་གྱུར་ཅིག

མི་མཐུན་པའི་ཕྱོགས་ཐམས་ཅད་ལས་རྣམ་པར་
རྒྱལ་ཞིང་བཀྲ་ཤིས་པར་གྱུར་ཅིག

སརྦ་མངྒ་ལཾ།

མི་མཐུན་པའི་ཕྱོགས
ཐམས་ཅད་ལས་རྣམ་པར་རྒྱལ་ཞིང་
བཀྲ་ཤིས་པར་གྱུར་ཅིག
མི་མཐུན་
པའི་ཕྱོགས་
ཐམས་ཅད་
ལས་རྣམ་པར་
རྒྱལ་ཞིང་
བཀྲ་ཤིས་
པར་གྱུར་ཅིག
མི་མཐུན་
པའི་ཕྱོགས་
ཐམས་ཅད་
ལས་རྣམ་པར་
རྒྱལ་ཞིང་
བཀྲ་ཤིས་
པར་གྱུར་ཅིག
མི་མཐུན་པའི་ཕྱོགས་ཐམས་ཅད་ལས་རྣམ་པར་
རྒྱལ་ཞིང་བཀྲ་ཤིས་པར་གྱུར་ཅིག
སརྦ་མངྒ་ལཾ།

བདེ་གཤེགས་ཐུགས་ཀྱི་བྱིན་རླབས་ལས། །ཕྱོགས་ལས་རྣམ་པར་རྒྱལ་གྱུར་ཅིག།